MW01222998

Among the Myrtle Trees

Restoring Abandoned Faith

Vanessa Crosson, R.N.

Scripture quotations marked NIV are taken from the *Holy Bible, New International Version®. NIV®.* Copyright © 1973, 1978, 1984 by International Bible Society. Used by permission of Zondervan. All rights reserved.

Additional scripture quotations marked GNT are taken from the Good News Translation — Second Edition. Copyright © 1992 by American Bible Society. Used by permission. All rights reserved.

FIRST EDITION

ISBN: 978-1-939748-45-4

Library of Congress Control Number: 2014930478

Published by
NewBookPublishing.com, a division of Reliance Media, Inc.
515 Cooper Commerce Drive, #140, Apopka, FL 32703
NewBookPublishing.com

Printed in the United States of America

Dedication

To those who have abandoned their faith: May you find the affirmation you so long for right here, right now. I pray that "Among the Myrtle Trees" gives you the encouragement and motivation to pick up the pieces of your life and run toward Jesus - the One who is the author and perfecter of faith.

To those who have helplessly witnessed a loved one question and abandon the faith that is only found in Jesus: I pray "Among the Myrtle Trees" helps you to better understand their struggle and activates you to be a strong source of prayer, love and support for them.

To those who have returned to their first love with Jesus Christ: You are a treasure of God's grace, mercy and love! I pray "Among the Myrtle Trees" will be a testament of your journey and spur you on to help others for such a time as this.

In honor of my mother, Sue Ellen Smith Cox, whose life continues to inspire me and nurture me even beyond her death.

Acknowledgements

To my husband, Trent: You are a rock and a constant source of strength for me. My emotional muscle would be saggy if I had not had you as my trainer and my companion in this journey. You have risked your life for God's will and for our family, literally. I know, without a shadow of doubt, that God gave me you. Together we have a vision and united we have a purpose in Him. I love you most.

To my children Nathaniel, Ava and Noah: You supported me and inspired me……oh, who am I kidding?! You were the ages of 7, 6 and 4 when the writing of "Among the Myrtle Trees" started and, naturally, you did not understand or help in any way. In fact, it got very messy, especially when your dad worked overseas. There were times when I just knew you were collaborating your efforts to team up against me! No apologies, though. I would be concerned if it were any different. It honors me to be your mother and it is you who drives me to be the best me that I can be. For your dad and me, it is our heart for you to SEE the Word of God lived out in our lives – not just hear it. May this book forever be a reminder and a token for you to always strive for God's perfect will for your lives no-matter the naysayers or the criticism. Keep your gaze on Him because all you will ever need is through Him.

To my Hosanna family: Thank you for praying and standing with me not only in times of strength but in times of weakness. You took me in and welcomed me back into the flock as if I had never been gone. You are truly a body of people bearing God's heart for the hurting and the broken. It is an honor to stand and serve alongside of you.

To my dad, Lee: Thank you for pushing me to dream and to never give up. It is because of you that I learned to care less of what others think and care more about my Heavenly Father and to lean on His understanding. I never thought I would say this…..but thank you for the "tough love". As a mom now, I realize that the groundings, chores, and spankings are harder on the parents and the kids actually get the reward from the discipline later on. Thank you for loving me hard and being a "softy" when it was required.

To my brother, Trever: Thank you for the contribution of your time and talent into the artwork for this book. I believe this is only the beginning for you. ~ Jeremiah 29:11 ~

To my Heavenly Father: My ultimate thanks are to You. There is no other that deserves the honor, glory, and praise that is due to You alone. Thank you for loving me when I am unlovable, being patient with me when I am unteachable, and SO forgiving when I feel that I am beyond forgiveness. But most of all, thank you for not abandoning me even when I was so quick to abandon You. I pray "Among the Myrtle Trees" is a blessing to others and that You receive honor and praise from it. I pray for broken relationships to be restored unto You and for redemption and peace that is only found in You to reign supreme.

Foreword

I have always been a person who desired things that are real. Vanessa, whom I have known since she was a teenager, has always been real. As one reads this book, one will find out what I have seen in her all these years. She has penned about her ups and downs in her journey. Like her, many may find themselves experiencing similar doubts, fears, and questions. Vanessa has beautifully addressed these things and has shown us how God has loved and sustained her through all of it. So this is a must-read for anyone experiencing heart-wrenching times. One will come to see that there is truly victory over them in Christ.

Dr. Jerry Lowery
Sr. Pastor Hosanna Christian Fellowship
Albertville, Alabama

Introduction

I remember sitting on the corner of my bed in a lamp-lit room when I was ten-years-old, feeling an overwhelming sense of insecurity and need. A deep hunger for significance pulled at my heart. I don't remember all the questions I asked my mom that night. I just remember talking through all the tears and longing for answers to some of life's deepest questions: "Why am I here? How were we created? What exactly did Jesus do for me? Why in the world did He do that?" My mom might not have felt prepared for my pop-quiz, but through her answers, I came to the knowledge of Christ and my need for Him. She prayed over me and walked me through the utterances of "God I need you. Thank you for what you did for me on the cross. Come into my heart." The aftermath of the questions, tears and emotion was humbling. I was surrounded by truth….His truth. Where I once felt insecure in the crazy world around me….I now feel secure in

Him. Hope lifted me. Grace embraced me. Purpose filled my heart and, through Christ, I received faith.

We all have our own stories. Each one involves diverse circumstances and different timing, but the same God. He offers and gives us all our very own version of "Amazing Grace." That one-on-one, personal experience with the Father cannot be drummed-up or duplicated. It is like our own "burning bush" experience that changes us from the inside out. We walk as best we know how on our new legs of faith, learning to trust and rely on Him more and more each day. The challenge today, just as it was in biblical times, is holding to that faith as strongly as the day you received it.

There are times in our lives that cause us to question every core truth we've ever known. This world we live in can weaken our faith, and personal tragedy can flat-out knock it into extinction. We start out singing "Blessed Assurance," then on down the winding road our tune changes to "It's A Hard Knock Life." Although the Israelites may have not known the words to those songs, they were defiantly singing to their own tune. They were God's "chosen people," but they certainly didn't feel like it. Because of their consistent disobedience to the One True God and refusal to listen to warnings through those whom God had sent, the Israelites found themselves overtaken by the Babylonian empire. They became prisoners of war in a foreign land for seventy....long....years. After surviving the exile and tumultuous ups and downs of returning to their homeland, they found themselves with a bad case of the spiritual doldrums. They struggled to find their significance and wrestled with their purpose – the same place that many of us find ourselves today.

But there's another place....a sweet spot in scripture to which we must go. This is the book of Zechariah, ironically positioned as the next-to-last chapter of the Old Testament, just before the New Testament begins. When the exile-born prophet shares his testimony, his intimate encounter with the Living God, it's as though he stutters and stammers as to report all that he saw, heard, felt and smelled. He repeats himself three times in seven sentences, saying "among the myrtle trees." The critic in me wants to take my red pen, mark out two of them and say, "Really, Zechariah? What kind of trees? Don't repeat yourself. We heard you the first time!" But I think Zechariah deserves some credit for, number one: not passing out, number two: taking it all in so that he would be able to convey the message to others, and number three: actually becoming a big boy and stepping up to be God's mouthpiece. Because, let's face it, those last two would have many of us doubting what we saw and heard and fearing what people might think of us.

So, here we have this imperfect guy who has a heavenly encounter. I can only imagine how everything looked to Zechariah, having known only a life of banishment. How green, lush and 3-D those trees must have been! Keep in mind, myrtles in that time and region, were very different from what we know as Crepe Myrtles today. They were one of the largest trees, with their width growing equal to their height and, of course, those eye-catching, star-like blooms to boot. With their sweet scent and lush beauty, myrtle trees were foretold in restoration prophesies as growing in places of briars and thriving in desolate places – which was a sign of the Lord's blessing on a cursed land (Isaiah 41:19/55:13). And these myrtles were just a symbol, a mere token, of the presence of Almighty God. They became a landmark of the places where God showed His overwhelming grace and His breathtaking faithfulness in the midst of the adulterous hearts of His people. They represented a place where God met His people right where they were: in the thick of hurt and healing, torn between fear and faith. He somehow, some way restored the deepest parts of their brokenness. Just as He did for them, He will do for us. Exactly what He offered to them, He offers to us. As Paul echoed, "Now to Him who is able to do immeasurably more than all we ask or imagine according to His power that is at work within us," let us go…. expectantly….among the myrtle trees.

Chapter 1

"You were running a good race. Who cut in on you to keep you from obeying the truth?" Galatians 5:7

"Man strays away into misery and pain, because he loses the sense of value and runs after the temporary and the trivial. He ignores the voice of God which warns and guides him from within; and he pays the penalty for his transgression."   *— Sri Sathya Sai Baba*

My husband always says, "I'm built for the fight, not for the run." For you to get as much amusement out of that as we do, I must share a few things with you. First of all, he's a police officer and both of those actions happen to fall within his job description. Secondly, he has a body frame comparable to…. well, let's not play the celebrity look-alike contest. A couple of his nicknames from friends are "Tank" and "Stump." That should help to give you a mental picture. And, lastly, have you ever seen muscle mass contend with speed? It's quite amusing. If not, think Looney Tunes: Abominable Snowman vs. Bugs Bunny.

And a little human physiology lesson here: Our bodies prepare us so that we can fight or run….or both. By gathering a lot of energy quickly, we are able to cope with threats to survival. This is known as the "fight or flight" mechanism. Whether it's a scary movie you have volunteered yourself to watch or something unplanned such as an accident or tragic news, your body responds to it. Stress hormones are released, the heart beats stronger and faster, breathing becomes more rapid, metabolism kicks up and the larger muscles receive more oxygenated blood. Your response can be automatic as well, just like a reflex reaction.

I'll share an example from my youth. It's a little embarrassing for me, but a good example none-the-less. I was sitting at a red light one night. Like a typical sixteen-year-old, I was counting how much time I had left until my curfew and I would turn into a pumpkin. I realized that I was behind one of my fellow classmates, but he didn't recognize me. In fact, he didn't even see me behind his pickup truck…..

until he backed into my car. Surprised and scared, I backed my little VW up, went around him, and drove home. (Not one of my better moments!) When I got home, I confessed the incident to my parents and received a tongue-lashing from my dad. Then off we went to make things right from my wrong decision. Thankfully, because my classmate was an honest guy with good parents, the experience didn't become any more painful, and it all worked out. "What was I thinking? I didn't do anything wrong! Why did I run? I should have just stayed put and called the police." Those were a few of my thoughts in the aftermath of my escape from the situation. It's easy to play Monday morning quarterback when you are able to stand back, look at the whole picture and think it out with no time constraints. But when it comes down to reacting quickly, we act as best as we know how using our experience and knowledge.

What can be said about our spiritual "fight or flight" response? In times when everything you know, trust and believe God for is tested – how do you react? For example, when you hit financial ruin – can you stand and believe that God works all things out for good for those who love Him? When you watch your sick child fight for his or her life – can you remain assured that God is in control? When you have been abused, neglected or abandoned – can you believe that God is a compassionate and loving God? Maybe your faith endures the fight for a certain amount of time, and then you find yourself running. Don't worry, there's a pretty good running club to join. Moses, one of the first members, ran out of guilt after killing an Egyptian. Fear kept him hidden for forty years. After experiencing victory against Jezebel, Elijah ran. In fear and exhaustion, he retreated thinking His luck with God was wearing out. Jonah, the president of our running club (mostly because of the whale incident), ran in disobedience to God. Because he felt the savage people of Nineveh were beyond redemption, he didn't want to be God's messenger of hope. And let's not forget that the Israelites, in the days of Zechariah, had become a generation of runners. They had turned their backs, plugged their ears and hardened their hearts toward God.

There was a time when I grew faith and held onto it for the sake of my mother's life. I can honestly say that it was the first incident in my sheltered life that required any faith at all and I felt sure that God would not disappoint my newfound confidence. When my mom was thirty-five, she had a mole removed in her doctor's office. After a pathology report revealed it to be cancerous, she underwent surgery to ensure that all of the malignancy had been removed. Life picked up from there and moved on to what you would call normal for the next six years. Then, during my sophomore year of high school, she had some health issues and it was determined that the melanoma was back. It returned with a vengeance. I watched my mom's health quickly deteriorate due to the rapidly growing cancer and the chemotherapy and radiation treatments she underwent to fight it.

At the age of forty-two, she dropped to a weight of eighty-five pounds, with visible tumors all over her body. Faith in God's healing was the only thing that could save my mom from her failing body; nothing else was working. God was our only hope. I was with her on several occasions when she became unresponsive. The last time it happened was at the hospital. A nurse's aide was also in the room, and she flipped the blue code switch. When they arrived, hospital staff members rushed me out so they could resuscitate my mom. I called several family members to come to the hospital and we paced outside the door praying, believing and trusting God for her healing. Nothing I heard and saw was positive, but I did not allow that to shake my faith. I prayed harder and cried out louder to God. After a very long attempt to revive her, the code was ended and she was pronounced dead. The staff members let us go in and visit her post-mortem.

My dad and I stood on opposite sides of my mom, who was stretched out flat on a pulled-apart hospital bed. Her room looked very different, as if she had been moved to a different one. I reached under the white sheet to hold her hand, but its cold temperature was too much of a reality to bear. I looked over and saw my dad crouched down over her face, uttering one last prayer, and felt an immediate shift in my heart. My faith turned to fear. My hope was crushed. And, my trust? Well, I had none – not even in God. The night I watched my mom die instead of seeing me off to my senior prom, was the night I laid my faith down, turned my back on God and ran. It's ironic, really. My faith was introduced with my mom at my bedside and it came to a screeching halt with me at her hospital bedside.

Sometimes, running is the only thing we know how to do. Spiritual suffering and fear can snowball into a whole gamut of emotions. We start rationalizing everything and trying to understand the tragedy that surrounds us. "God must not love me; otherwise, He wouldn't have allowed this to happen." Better yet: "He must not exist." Scared, angry and hurt, we run as fast as we can, abandoning the God we feel has abandoned us. Not many can relate to running – and those who can have a hard time admitting it or recognizing it….as I once did. It's not something we tend to be proud of, not a trophy engraved with WINNER: FASTEST RUNNER FROM GOD to be displayed in our houses. So, as welcoming as those myrtle trees are, it would be an injustice to jump ahead without first pulling the bandages off the hurts and wounds we've covered up and hidden within our broken hearts in order to protect ourselves.

In other words, we must uncover our deepest grievances and disappointments, allowing God to work within us. It is then that we realize our quest to find fulfillment and healing from all other sources has failed, leaving us empty. He allowed the run to reveal that He is the only One that can restore our faith. He is the author and finisher of our faith. We must embrace the freedom by understanding that there is no tragedy and nothing to be ashamed of in running. The only tragedy would be *not* returning to THE ONLY ONE to whom we can and should run. It is in the run we are assured that nothing can separate us from God's love. Upon discovering that in the run He builds us up for the fight, we realize the whole time we have been running….it's been in the palm of His hand.

Prayer ~ God, I come to You as a runner, not knowing who I am anymore and not knowing You like I thought I once did. Are You there? I need to know that You are. I need to feel the warmth of You in my cold heart. I have run and hid and concealed my deepest hurts until I can do it no longer. I am tired – I need a strength that only You can give. I am lonely – I need the companionship that is only found in You. I have run for so long that it has become all I know. Begin now, God, a work of restoration in my heart. Show me how to walk with You. Pick me up, God, and carry me. I am tired of running. ~ Amen ~

Shades of Scripture

"The Spirit clearly says that in later times some will abandon the faith and follow deceiving spirits and things taught by demons." 1 Timothy 4:1

"I had planted you like a choice vine of sound and reliable stock. How then did you turn against me into a corrupt, wild vine?" Jeremiah 2:21

"The Lord says: "What accusation did your ancestors bring against me? What made them turn

away from me? They worshipped worthless idols and became worthless themselves." Jeremiah 2:5

"Holding faith and a good conscience. By rejecting this, some have made shipwreck of their faith" 1 Timothy 1:19

"But they quickly forgot what he had done and acted without waiting for his advice. They were filled with craving in the desert and put God to the test." Psalm 106:13-14

"If you do not stand firm in your faith, you will not stand at all." Isaiah 7:9

Chapter 2

"But I have this against you that you have abandoned the love you had at first." Revelation 2:4

"Your faith will not fail while God sustains it; you are not strong enough to fall away while God is resolved to hold you."
— *J.I. Packer*

I would rather have swum with sharks wearing a chum suit than to have written this chapter. That's just being honest. I was truly not looking forward to it at all. First of all, my hesitancy was due to the fact that I didn't want this chapter to come across like a pointed finger, for me to be labeled a "Bible banger" or, worse yet, for the chapter to have a doomsday feel to it. That is because I don't believe that is God's heart at all. Secondly, I had to reveal some things about my past that I wasn't too crazy about sharing. I felt a huge conviction as I tip-toed around it, realizing that it is an injustice to the restoration process not to visit our reasons for abandoning our faith. We must bring our darkness into His light.

Let's think back to where we first heard the Word of God. Well, back up a little bit more....what *is* the Word of God? John 1: 1-2 tells us: "In the beginning was the Word, and the Word was with God, and the Word was God. He was with God in the beginning." That can be a bit of a tongue-twister if you read it fast enough. Hop on down to John 1:14 as John the apostle breaks it down more: "The Word became flesh and made His dwelling among us. We have seen His glory, and the glory of the One and Only, who came from the Father, full of grace and truth." The Word of God is Jesus. Also, it refers to the Bible. 2 Timothy 3:16 tells us that "all scripture is God-breathed and is useful for teaching, rebuking, correcting and training in righteousness." So, basically, the Word of God is Jesus; it is the written word given to us about Jesus and it is, in the very essence, truth.

Now, let's think back to when we first heard the truth about Jesus, and about being saved. I've already shared *my* experience in the Introduction. It's your turn to remember all the whos, whats, whens and wheres of your receiving the

Word of God. How old were you? Where were you? Who was with you? And, one more, *how* did you receive it?

The Bible also describes the Word of God as being "living and active" (Hebrews 4:12) and a "lamp unto our feet and a light unto our path" (Psalm 119:105). Then why in the world do we feel like dead people walking around in the dark? Let's look at what Jesus says about hearing the word. In Luke 8:5-10, Jesus tells the parable of the sower. He talks about a farmer scattering seed to grow. Jesus goes on to describe how the seed fell to different parts of the ground and how it was received. Some seed was quickly snatched and eaten by birds. The other seed fell among rocks or thorns or onto clear, ready soil. I really appreciate how Jesus goes on to explain the meaning of His teaching for people like me:

"This is the meaning of the parable: The seed is the Word of God. Those along the path are the ones who hear, and then the devil comes and takes away the word from their hearts, so that they may not believe and be saved. Those on the rock are the ones who receive the word with joy when they hear it, but they have no root. They believe for a while, but in the time of testing they fall away. The seed that fell among the thorns stands for those who hear, but as they go on their way they are choked by life's worries, riches and pleasures,

and they do not mature. But the seed on good soil stands for those with a noble and good heart, who hear the word, retain it, and by persevering produce a crop." Luke 8:11-15

There is so much revelation in this verse! I received the word with joy, but fell away in my time of testing. I was on the rocks. Where are you? Has the testing of this life caused you to fall away from the truth? Are the worries, riches and pleasures of this life choking out God's Word for you?

Wherever you are, reassure yourself with this fact: NOTHING can separate you from the love that GOD has for YOU. Saul was not only the preacher of this message, but also the living proof. Speaking of rocks, Saul was as solid as they come when it came to the persecution against Christians. He was like the Grinch of the Bible days, but instead of his heart being two sizes too small, it was made of stone. It was when Saul encountered God's Word that his stony heart was cultivated into the God-fearing, Jesus-serving Apostle Paul that we know. In 1 Corinthians 3, Paul shares information about their teaching and ministering to others and he refers to it as "planting seed" with others coming along and "watering" the seed. He goes on to give credit where it is due:

"The one who plants and the one who waters really do not matter. It is God who matters because he makes the plant grow." 1 Corinthians 3:7

The Elephant Among the Rocks

Let's just go ahead and acknowledge the elephant in the room....or, rather, among the rocks.

"For how can those who abandon their faith be brought back to repent again? They were once in God's light; they tasted heaven's gift and received their share of the Holy Spirit; they knew from experience that God's word is good, and they had felt the powers of the coming age. And then they abandoned their faith! It is impossible to bring them back to repent again, because they are again crucifying the Son of God and exposing him to public shame." Hebrews 6:4-6

That verse kicked me square in the face. Talk about conviction – there it is. The thought of me nailing Jesus to that cross over and over again because of my abandonment was a conviction that I could no longer bear. The writer of Hebrews, although unknown, speaks much revelatory truth in those two verses. It is said that the book of Hebrews was written to the members of the early church who, because of imprisonment and oppression, were inclined to go back to their previous way of life and abandon their newfound faith and privilege in Christ Jesus. I like how the Quest Study Bible introduces the book of Hebrews as "something like a coach's pep talk at halftime: It can help us find the inspiration to keep on going in the faith, and it can warn us of the dangers of defeat." (Quest Study Bible – Zondervan)

I don't want to come across as arguing or justifying around this verse, because it is God-breathed and it is what brought me to a turnaround point. But let's break this verse down and digest it for ourselves. Maybe, sometimes, when some of us are first saved, we receive head knowledge of God's Word but never really "taste heaven's gift" or "share of the Holy Spirit." Maybe we haven't reached that point in our life yet that we can say from experience that "God's Word is good." Those aren't revelations which necessarily happen overnight, or after an "Amen" from our prayers. God reveals Himself in different ways at different times in our lives to each of us. I know for sure, when I decided to give up on God at the age of eighteen, that I had not felt the powers of the coming age. Maybe all of that comes through our trials and testing, and that's why God allows it. I think a lot of times we give up on God before any of that good stuff ever happens and we close our hearts to its reality when it does happen. Perhaps it takes having our own Adam or Eve experience to taste the sin for ourselves before we can fully appreciate the saving grace of our Savior.

An intermission disclaimer: The above paragraph and

the ones to follow may challenge some religious foundations and beliefs. I do not, nor will I ever, claim to be an expert Theologian. You will never, EVER hear me say that someone is wrong in their beliefs, no matter what they are. I feel that a conviction of such beliefs is a work that only God can do. You will, however, hear me toss thoughts around and ask questions. Thus, the many "maybes", "perhaps", and "I think's" in the previous paragraph. My heart is simply to share the rockiest part of my life and what I feel God revealed to me in that tough time. Maybe God has you in a similar place and maybe you are trying to make sense of it all.

Let's go back to Paul. As Saul, a leader against the persecution against Christians, how many seeds of God's Word had fallen among the rocks of his heart in his interactions with the Christians he led to their punishment? How often would truth and prayer be spoken out loud against him as he bound their hands to arrest them? Yet, Saul's heart would remain cold and resistant. It took God's divine intervention for Saul's physical eyes to be closed and the eyes of his heart to be opened. Only God could bring about such a testimony from someone like Paul:

"Even though I was once a blasphemer and a persecutor and a violent man, I was shown mercy because I acted in

ignorance and unbelief. The grace of our Lord was poured out on me abundantly, along with the faith and love that are in Christ Jesus." 1 Timothy 1:13-14

It took Saul being blinded for Paul to see. It took Saul being lost for Paul to be found. Maybe that's what Hebrews 6:4-6 refers to – for someone such as Paul to have the experience that he did and to then have abandoned his faith and return with a heart of Saul. 1 Peter 3:18 assures, "For Christ died for sins once and for all." The sacrifice of Christ was and is sufficient.

I know there are many opinions regarding salvation and there is a constant war between each belief of salvation versus predestination. Regardless of where you stand and even where I stand on that subject, let's lay it down. I tend to agree with Paul:

"Remind your people of this, and give them a solemn warning in God's presence not to fight over words. It does no good, but only ruins the people who listen. Do your best to win full approval in God's sight, as a worker who is not ashamed of his work, one who correctly teaches the message of God's truth. Keep away from profane and foolish discussions, which only drive people farther away from God." 2 Timothy 2:14-16

Am I saying that our salvation or our beliefs are not important? Certainly not. A wall of segregation exists between both ideas of salvation and predestination. I challenge you to knock that wall down. In order for you to do that, I encourage you to drop personal boundaries of belief and simply focus on Him. It can become something else to be tangled in if we put too much emphasis on "what" we are rather than "who" we are in Him. If we form our thinking around one idea or one belief about our relationship with God, then we can miss the bigger picture.

Why would I suggest such a thing? You see, for a long time, I reassured myself with the idea that because I had prayed the sinner's prayer when I was ten-years-old, everything was okay. I excused myself from a need for God due to the fact that I had "taken care of that," as if "being saved" had been checked off my Bucket List. It's done. It's over. I'm moving on. All the while, God was cultivating my heart and stirring me to a conviction of my broken covenant with Him. This is a diluted way to view our relationship with Christ. The same thing can happen if we look to predestination as our eternal security. A certain passivity can take place when we treat it like a High School Exit Exam – take it, pass it, done. However, Jesus defined the need for our relationship to be an "abiding" relationship: To abide is to remain, to continue and to stay. Abide is an action verb, not a passive one.

"Remain in me, and I will remain in you. No branch can bear fruit by itself; it must remain in the vine. Neither can you bear fruit unless you remain in me." John 15:4

It takes effort to withstand and endure without submitting or abandoning our faith. I believe that's what Paul meant by saying, "working out your salvation" in Philippians 2:12. Not that it was in boisterous works to display in hopes for God's approval. But, rather, it was a constant and daily exchange with the Heavenly Father. It doesn't matter how we got there, what matters is that we stay. HE alone is our salvation. HE is the One who determines our destiny.

Testing...One, Two

It is when we find ourselves in our deepest desperation, alone and hurting, that we learn what we are truly made of. Times of testing are not for God but of God. Even when we have gotten ourselves into the worst of predicaments, God truly does work through those things, drawing us closer to Him. Throughout the books of Isaiah and Jeremiah, God sent warning after warning for the people to turn back to Him. When the Israelites continued in disobedience, God allowed

Babylon to be an instrument of judgment upon them. God's people were moved from their homeland to no man's land. Even in the face of discipline, God always announced his mercy in their restoration. He sees the good in us even when all that we and everybody else sees is the bad. As the people were taken captive, banished from their homes and split-up from their families, God came to Jeremiah and comforted him. When Jeremiah walked past the temple, he saw two baskets of figs: one was filled with good figs and the other with bad ones. This is what God told him:

"Then the word of the Lord came to me: "This is what the Lord, the God of Israel, says: 'Like these good figs, I regard as good the exiles from Judah, whom I sent away from this place to the land of the Babylonians. My eyes will watch over them for their good, and I will bring them back to this land. I will build them up and not tear them down; I will plant them and not uproot them. I will give them a heart to know me, that I am the Lord. They will be my people, and I will be their God, for they will return to me with all their heart." Jeremiah 24: 4-7

Notice that all the people were sent to exile. The good, the bad and the ugly all belonged to King Nebuchadnezzar. God did not put all the "good people" in a little bubble like we sometimes would like for Him to. They all faced the same consequences. Here's the kicker: even though they were all subject to this very hard time of testing, the outcome would be very different for some. Those that God considered "good" would not only survive the exile, but they would also thrive. God promised to watch over them and to bring them back. Instead of leaving them torn down every which way, He built them up.

Times of testing are no fun at all. Many times, we don't understand them. Sometimes, God gives us revelation after our trials so we can better understand them and appreciate them, but sometimes He doesn't. Maybe He has allowed you to pass through some very difficult times because, like Job, He is pleased with you. There's a lot we don't know and like about the tribulations of this life, but this we can be sure of: It is God's heart to watch over us for our good and to plant us. He wants to build us up and not tear us down. The perfect blood of Jesus was sacrificed to atone for the hardest of hearts and the rockiest of lives. He is the Judge and the Cultivator over our hearts and He knows what is in there and what is lacking. Only He knows if there is faith the size of a mustard seed among the rockiest of hearts. I hear He can work with that. His desire is to plant us and to not uproot us. He is, by the way, the Great Stone Roller. He sustains us through the rockiest of seasons and through our tough times, to soften our hearts and move us from among the rocks to a place among the myrtle trees.

Prayer ~ *God, only you know what's in my heart. You see things in me that I don't. You know me better than I know myself. Forgive me, God, for allowing my hard times and all the worries of this world to pull me away from You. I want to be rooted and grounded in You and to know your loving-kindness like never before. I want to truly come into the light of You. I want to taste and see for myself that You are good. Remove the rocks from my heart, God, and plant new life that is found in You deep within me. I want to experience You like never before. Help me to see you and to remain in you all the days of my life. Give me a heart to know you, God, and to return to you. I want to hear you say: "You are Mine." And I want to be able to say: "He is mine." ~ Amen ~*

Shades of Scripture

"Examine yourselves to see whether you are in the faith; test yourselves. Do you not realize that Christ Jesus is in you – unless, of course, you fail the test?" 2 Corinthians 13:5

"You deserted the Rock who fathered you; you forgot the God who gave you birth." Deuteronomy 32:18

"Remember how the Lord your God led you all the way in the wilderness these forty years, to humble and test you in order to know what was in your heart, whether or not you would keep his commands." Deuteronomy 8:2

"As for you, see that what you have heard from the beginning remains in you. If it does, you also will remain in the Son and in the Father." 1 John 2:24

"And I pray that Christ will make his home in your hearts through faith. I pray that you may have your roots and foundation in love, so that you, together with all God's people, may have the power to understand how broad and long, how high and deep, is Christ's love. Yes, may you come to know his love – although it can never be fully known – and so be completely filled with the very nature of God." Ephesians 3:17-19

"Keep your roots deep in him, build your lives on him, and become stronger in your faith, as you were taught. And be filled with thanksgiving."
Colossians 2:7

"To give to those who mourn in Zion, Joy and gladness instead of grief, a song of praise instead of sorrow. They will be like trees that the LORD himself has planted. They will all do what is right, and God will be praised for what he has done."
Isaiah 61:3

Chapter 3

"But the One who will rescue them is strong – his name is the Lord Almighty. He himself will take up their cause and bring peace to the earth, but trouble to the people of Babylonia." Jeremiah 50:34

"The fundamental story arc of the Bible is God is passionate about rescuing this world, restoring it, renewing it." — *Rob Bell*

On the outside there appeared to be life, but the inside was dead. At times, depression would be so heavy that it felt as if a thought process was required to keep breathing. The anguish was overwhelming. Breathe in. Breathe out. It felt as if staying alive took too much effort and that dying would be easier. My life continued on, but it felt meaningless.

This was me. I was officially "the one" – the one sheep that wandered away. Since I felt that God had failed me in my mother's death, I chose to go my own way. I made my own plans and chose my own direction without giving any thought to God. My last prayers of crying out for my mom's life felt like they bounced right back, so I stopped praying. Going to church felt pointless, so I didn't go. I quit looking for Him. I stopped searching for Him. As if I had uncovered some sort of childhood myth, the Bible was moved from the coffee table and stored in the closet with the Easter Bunny and Santa Clause. I figured that no one could hurt me if I didn't allow them to get close enough – including God. Working at the hospital and attending nursing school, along with my recent marriage had my full attention that first year after my mom passed. I poured myself into anything and everything that would get my mind off of my personal pain. I craved a degree, a nice house and a perfect little white picket fence marriage to fill the space where God once was. Yes, regretfully, I was that one.

This is right where the enemy wants you. Oh, yeah, Satan is real. He is as real as God is. Until that glorious day that God shuts him up into his fiery pit for eternity, he walks about on this earth with you and me. Jesus warned us of that fact. Paul cautioned us to "be alert, be on watch! Your enemy, the Devil, roams around like a roaring lion, looking for someone to devour." Satan feeds off of our weaknesses and hurts and he anticipates an easy kill because of it. That's why when Jesus fasted for forty-days and forty-nights, the enemy tried so hard to work against Him when He was alone, experiencing extreme hunger and parching thirst. It's no different for us. Satan's tactics have not changed. When you are hurting and feel alone, when it feels like the wrongest of wrongs has been committed against you, he is the one who will attempt to use that as a wedge between you and your Creator.

The enemy will tell you that the love and healing you need and look for will not occur because God does not exist. When you are grieving from the deepest of heartaches, he is the one that will tell you that if there is a God, He must not love you because of all the bad things that have happened to you. I know this, because these are the lies that I believed for too long. I allowed Satan to kick me while I was down and I just laid there and took it. If you find yourself in a similar situation, questioning God's existence and His love for you, ask yourself: "Am I doubting God's existence because of my uncomfortable circumstances? Do I question God's love for me because I don't feel loved or lovable at this juncture in my life?" If the answer to either one of those is a "yes," then you can bet your crown in Heaven that the enemy is trying to use your situation and your emotions to contradict your faith. Satan doesn't want you to experience God, especially at a time when you need God the most. He knows doing that will make a believer out of you.

Many of us grew up learning the classic Bible stories from Sunday school, if we weren't raised in church, then what we know and learned of God is either from the testimonies of others or our own obtained biblical research and ideas we have just picked up here and there. We get glimpses of God through the combination of it all. This sometimes can impress a fairy-tale view of God within us because we have only heard about Him and are mesmerized by the idea of Him, but have never experienced Him. I think that many times, we do experience Him, but we just don't have the spiritual eyes to see Him. Throughout the Bible, God declares in His messages to the people: "those who have ears, let him hear!" In teaching the parables, Jesus said: "those who have eyes, let him see!" We have lots of head knowledge, but no heart knowledge. God is a God of personal experience. He is a God of encounter who desires intimacy with His children. He is the Creator of heaven and earth and all living things and has paved the way, through Jesus Christ, so that He may have minute-by-minute connection with us all. Crazy, you say? Don't let your earthly mindset contradict the earth-shaking, veil-ripping, death-defeating love that God expresses for you.

Throughout the Bible, God expressed His "jealousy" over His people. And this is not a jealousy like the envy that you or I would experience. For God, it is described and used interchangeably with being zealous. It's descriptive of His protective nature over His people as a whole and as individuals. It's amazing how God loves all and loves one. And how He can be both everywhere and also in just one place in His omnipresence is mind-blowing. That's what makes Him the ONE and the ONLY. Jesus described the Godly love for the one in this parable:

"Suppose one of you has a hundred sheep and loses one of them—what do you do? You leave the other ninety-nine sheep in the pasture and go looking for the one that got lost until you find it. When you find it, you are so happy that you put it on your shoulders and carry it back home. Then you call your friends and neighbors together and say to them, 'I am so happy I found my lost sheep. Let us celebrate!' In the same way, I tell you, there will be more joy in heaven over one

sinner who repents than over ninety-nine respectable people who do not need to repent." Luke 15:4-7

God is real. "You believe that there is one God. Good! Even the demons believe that – and shudder." (James 2:19) He's the One that goes after one. We don't deserve that kind of rescue, but His mercy reaches beyond our habit to stray away from Him. That is what God's message was to Zechariah among those myrtles. Apart from the Israelites' repetitive history of defiance, God was the One to bring them back. In the same breath of His announcement of discipline, He promised to rescue them. A promise is one thing. But to receive the promise is a whole separate affinity. That's where the personal encounter comes in. When God does what He says He's going to do – things get real. When His strength overcomes your weaknesses, when your heart is healed in His forgiveness, when you actually feel the moment God finds you….the lid pops off of your box of make-believe. He has a way of blowing the hinges off your closet of fairy-tales.

God, in His power and out-stretched-hand, has a way of redefining real. Not that He has anything to prove to anyone, but if it's reality you need, He is THE ONE to give it. When God showed up among the myrtle trees, the Israelites were at their highest peak of doubt and disbelief. He went to them not because they had asked or necessarily prayed, but because that's how God is. He is faithful in the midst of our faithlessness. When the Israelites were as lost sheep, God found them among the myrtle trees. He is our Rescuer and He delights to find us, lift us up and carry us on His shoulders. The genuine, proven, one true God finds us right where we are, among the myrtle trees or not. Call out to the One.

Prayer ~ *Oh, Heavenly Father, I don't know where I am but I am thankful You do. Find me, God. I feel lost and alone and separated from You. Rescue me, God. I am the one that has strayed away. I have experienced the torment and listened to lies of the one who seeks to destroy me. Forgive me, God. Thank you for your promises to comfort, to rescue and to restore. I long for a personal encounter with You. Embrace me, God, and place me on your shoulder. I so desperately long to experience the heavenly joy and celebration that You have for me.* ~ *Amen* ~

Shades of Scripture

"I will show my love to the one I called 'Not my loved one.' I will say to those called 'Not my people,' 'You are my people,' and they will say, 'You are my God.'" Hosea 2:23

"How terrible for the world that there are things that make people lose their faith! Such things will happen – but how terrible for the one who causes them!" Matthew 18:7

"Because of the increase of wickedness, the love of most will grow cold, but the one who stands firm to the end will be saved." Matthew 24:12-13

"Who is it that overcomes the world? Only the one who believes that Jesus is the Son of God." 1 John 5:5

"I am surprised at you! In no time at all you are deserting the one who called you by the grace of Christ, and are accepting another gospel." Galatians 1:6

"Jesus answered, "What God wants you to do is to believe in the one he sent." John 6:29

"Those who accept my commandments and obey them are the ones who love me. My Father will love those who love me; I too will love them and reveal myself to them." John 14:21

Chapter 4

REMEMBRANCE

"Remember this, you sinners; consider what I have done. Remember what happened long ago; acknowledge that I alone am God and that there is no one else like me."
Isaiah 46:8-9

"Unless we remember we cannot understand."
— E.M. Forster

I can picture two grandparents sitting fireside with their grandchildren, reminiscing about the "good old days" and how things used to be. The kids are enjoying being the listeners just as much as the "grands" are enjoying being the tellers. "One more! One more!" chant the rowdy kids on a sugar high from roasted marshmallows.

"Okay, okay – just ONE more," says the grandmother.

"I'll tell you the one I was told to never forget, one that is to be passed down from generation to generation. So, you need to be sure to tell..." she pauses. Then, with a wrinkled brow and a confused expression, she turns to her husband and asks, "I should have started with that one, huh? You're supposed to keep me straight. You're good at that you know."

"Go on, already!" encourages the eldest and most eager of the brood. And the granddad helps lead the conversation in the right direction: "My great granddad told me about him and his family moving from Egypt when he was ten-years-old. His parents were slaves. Back then, if you were anything other than an Egyptian, you were a slave to one."

The grandmother interrupts, "Don't forget we all have to get up early in the morning. That cotton's not going to pick itself." The granddad makes a funny face as if he is reprogramming the story to the shorter version.

He starts again, saying, "Pharaoh was a bad king. He was as bad as they come. He wouldn't let God's people free."

The grandmother jumps in to take over. "Are we gonna talk about Pharaoh or are we gonna talk about God? God promised He would deliver them and take care of them and that He did! As they were traveling out of Egypt, Pharaoh's army was given orders to capture them. When they reached the Red Sea, God actually parted the waters so they could walk through on dry ground."

One of the grandchildren pops up and asks, "Whoa! God can do that?!"

"Yes," answers the grandfather. "God did do that and still can. My great granddad said that they all were amazed how they could walk between two walls of water and not get a drop of water on them."

By this time both grandparents are comfortable taking turns in sharing, so the grandmother takes hers. "My grandpop told me that they didn't know where they were going, so God led them with a cloud by day and fire by night. When they needed to stop and rest the cloud and fire would stop also. The presence of God was with them the whole time and never left them."

"And the manna," adds the grandfather. "They woke up to this frost-looking stuff on the ground and it was manna for them to eat." The intrigued children wanted to know if it was good and what it tasted like, so the grandfather quickly answers, "They said it was a sweet-tasting honey bread. God gave them fresh manna every morning for them to eat."

"I remember seeing the manna in a jar at my great grandparents' house," recollects the grandmother. "I'd give anything if I knew where that jar is now," she adds remorsefully.

Something has happened. We don't hear stories like this anymore. Too many generations have passed now since God popped the wheels off the chariots of Pharaoh's army. God showed up and showed out so many times on behalf of His people. The only way we know about it now is from reading about it in the Bible. The Israelites were encouraged to not let a memory lapse occur.

"Only be careful, and watch yourselves closely so that you do not forget the things your eyes have seen or let them fade from your heart as long as you live. Teach them to your children and to their children after them." Deuteronomy 4:9

What has happened? Has too much time passed? Did the ball get dropped from one generation to another? We need to remember that people have a tendency to be forgetful. Today, just to be sure we remember, we have electronic reminders that remind us to remember. As the phrase for this generation goes – "There's an app for that." You've got your standard alerts you can set on your smartphone or you can take it a step further. There are birthday reminders, fasting reminders, check-in reminders for your hotel or airline, medicine reminders, doctor's appointment reminders and bill reminders. I think it's safe to say that we are a people that need to be reminded. Our forgetting is not necessarily intentional. It's fair to say that distraction is the number one culprit, right next to an innocent absentmindedness. We are constantly distracted in this busy world with temptations all around, changing our focus and tripping over our own purposes. We become discouraged in the throes of it all, and a sort of spiritual amnesia occurs.

This doesn't take our Creator by surprise. In fact, "remembering" is mentioned in the Bible over two hundred and sixty times. Throughout the Old and New Testaments, God constantly reminds His people of His commandments, promises, provisions and presence. Sometimes, God sends His sticky note reminders through other people, leaders and His disciples. For instance, in Deuteronomy, there was a lot of remembering going on. God's people, being led by Moses, had forty years of wilderness and preparation behind them and a flooding river with a land of giants ahead. Talk about being between a rock and a hard place! They found themselves suspended between two worlds: the not-so-fun Egypt behind them and ahead of them, the unpaved, unfamiliar road to this "promised land" they kept hearing about. It was definitely one of those "Are we there yet?" moments. (This brings to mind some hiking experiences with my kids.) They were stuck and required constant reminding from Moses and from themselves, that God had taken care of them to that point and He would continue to take care of them until they reached their land of promise.

"Then beware, lest you forget the LORD who brought you out of the land of Egypt, from the house of bondage." *Deuteronomy 6:12*

Fast-forward about nine hundred years to the days of Zechariah. God's people had been released by King Cyrus after being held captive in Babylon for seventy years. Many of them were born into bondage, never seeing their homeland of Jerusalem or experiencing freedom. They set about their purpose and relationship with God with passion and conviction, like that of a born-again believer. No sooner than they put up their tents, they were faced with hindrance, temptation, and hardship. Good feelings were gone. Enduring the opposition of neighboring people, famine and poverty, the people could not see how their circumstances had improved from Babylon. They became disheartened and their confidence in God was failing. Twenty years had passed since their release to "freedom," and they were in as much, if not more, bondage in their homeland as they were when they lived in exile. They had forgotten where they had been and the God who got them through. They also forgot where they were going and the only One who could help them get there. Can you relate? I sure can.

When God remembers, He doesn't just have passing thoughts. Things happen. He responds in mercy and shows compassion. When God remembered Noah and his family on the ark, He sent a wind over the earth and the waters receded. When God's people went into battle, He gave instructions for them to sound a trumpet and, at that time, He rescued them from their enemies. When God remembered Rachel and Hannah, He enabled them to conceive. When the cities of Sodom and Gomorrah were destroyed, God removed Lot from the catastrophe because He remembered Abraham. As Jesus hung in crucifixion alongside two criminals, one said: "Jesus, remember me when you come into your kingdom." Jesus replied, "I tell you the truth, today you will be with me in paradise."

It is when God remembers that His love and compassion are experienced in a mighty way. Was it a coincidence that Zechariah's name means "Yahweh remembers"? No. There are no coincidences with God. God chose to move through Zechariah to remind His people of His purpose for them beyond the restored temple and to motivate them. Before the people could grasp what God had in store for them, they first had to remember. It was vital for them to remember how God had poured manna from the sky and water from rocks. He wanted them to remember how He guided them day and night and never left their side.

We need to remember. Like the Israelites of Zechariah's time, we have become discouraged, distracted and beaten down from what is behind us and overcome with fear and timidity about what is ahead. It is when we remember God that things start coming back into proper focus. Distractions, temptations, discouragement, defeat – they all get smaller. God gets bigger when we remember Him. When we identify Him as the Almighty God that He is, a certain celebration takes place within our hearts. Remembering then becomes for us more than just a passing thought; it becomes a sincere act of worship. When we stop and take notice of God and all the things He has done for and given to us, especially in the times when we least deserve it, it is honor to Him. We must forget all those things that cause us to forget Him and put Him first. It is when we center our remembrance on WHO WAS AND IS AND IS TO COME that our faith arises.

Prayer ~ *God, how could I forget you?   Awaken and refresh my memory of You, Father. Help me to recognize You in a greater way so I can never, ever forget you again. Take all distractions and hindrances that cause me to forget what is important: YOU. God, I know that when my focus is on You that my purpose and path become clearer. Like Habakkuk, I pray "Oh Lord, I have heard of what you have done and I am filled with awe. Now do again in our times the great deeds you used to do. Be merciful, even when you're angry." Forgive me, God, for forgetting how great and awesome You are. And most of all, thank You, for remembering me in spite of my forgetfulness. ~ Amen ~*

Shades of Scripture

"Does a young woman forget her jewelry or a bride her wedding dress? But my people have forgotten me for more days than be counted." Jeremiah 2:32

"They refused to obey; they forgot all you did; they forgot the miracles you had performed. In their pride they chose a leader to take them back to slavery in Egypt. But you are a God who forgives; you are gracious and loving, slow to be angry.

Your mercy is great, you did not forsake them." Nehemiah 9:17

"Do not remember the sins of my youth and my rebellious ways; according to your love remember me, for you, Lord, are good." Psalm 25:7

"I will remember the deeds of the Lord; yes, I will remember your miracles of long ago." Psalm 77:11

"The Lord is our God; his commands are for all the world. Never forget God's covenant, which he made to last forever." 1 Chronicles 16:14-15

"Then those who feared the Lord talked with each other, and the Lord listened and heard. A scroll of remembrance was written in his presence concerning those who feared the Lord and honored his name." Malachi 3:16

"Do not merely listen to the word, and so deceive yourselves. Do what it says. Anyone who listens to the word but does not do what it says is like someone who looks at his face in a mirror and, after looking

at himself, goes away and immediately forgets what he looks like. But whoever looks intently into the perfect law that gives freedom, and continues in it—not forgetting what they have heard, but doing it—they will be blessed in what they do." James 1:22-25

Chapter 5

"But even now," says the Lord, "repent sincerely and return to me with fasting and weeping and mourning. Let your broken heart show your sorrow; tearing your clothes is not enough." Come back to the Lord your God. He is kind and full of mercy; he is patient and keeps his promise; he is always ready to forgive and not punish." Joel 2:12-13

In the South, we value our traditions. In fact, it's a tradition to have traditions and lots of them. Most of them revolve around the Three F's: Football, Food and Family. We swap recipes like they are business cards and if you don't have any sweet tea chilling in the fridge, that is reason enough to call off a gathering. Traditions remind us of who we are and where we come from. Our traditions rise from our culture, giving roots to our heritage with meaning and significance.

Imagine being invited somewhere and asked not to dress the way you usually dress or to behave in a different manner than usual. Sort of like, "Hey, come watch the football game with us, but just wear a white t-shirt and blue jeans. Don't bother wearing your team attire or cheering for your team." Your friends actually went to the trouble to mail you an invitation, along with a reminder email and a text. And when they didn't hear from you, they took the time to call you. In that conversation, they tell you how much they would like for you to come and say it wouldn't be the same without you there. Are you honored to accept the invitation? Or do you turn down the invitation because they have requested a few conditions?

In a similar fashion, God invited the Israelites back to Him. The book of Zechariah opens with a call to return. This call was an invitation signaling that it was time. God was calling His people back to Him. The Invitation read as follows:

The LORD Almighty told Zechariah to say to the people, "I, the LORD, was very angry with your ancestors, but now I say to you, 'Return to me, and I will return to you. Do not be like your ancestors. Long ago the prophets gave them my message, telling them not to live evil, sinful lives any longer. But they would not listen to me or obey me. Your ancestors and those prophets are no longer alive. Through my servants the prophets I gave your ancestors commands and warnings, but they disregarded them and suffered the consequences. Then they repented and acknowledged that I, the LORD Almighty, had punished them as they deserved and as I had determined to do.'" Zechariah 1: 2-6

This invitation came to Zechariah about three months before he experienced God among the myrtle trees. God was not only calling them back to Him through repentance, He was also asking them to return in a way they had not necessarily been taught or seen demonstrated by their ancestors. Commonly, we look up to our parents or certain family members and aspire to walk in their footsteps. In this case, God was calling them to start fresh and break tradition. This was not one of those "obey your father and your mother" teachings. In fact, it was the opposite. Everything that the previous generation did led them down a path of destruction. What had become their traditional way of life no longer represented who they were as God's people. For their survival and their betterment, God was being the Ultimate Father and teaching them the way they should go.

It wasn't necessarily that their ancestors did wrong or sinned. God's biggest issue with the previous generation was this:

"But my people stubbornly refused to listen. They closed their minds and made their hearts as hard as rock. Because they would not listen when I spoke, I did not answer when they prayed." Zechariah 7:11-13

They wouldn't listen. The previous generation was a very stubborn, very hard-hearted generation.

Our oldest son, Nathaniel, has always been very easy to discipline. When he was learning to walk, naturally, he would pull up on things. One day, I caught him using one of the long, panel curtains in the living room to pull himself up with. I looked above him and the heavy, wrought iron rod was angled to hit him in the head. I ran over to him, gave him a very stern look and said "No!" He had never seen me make a face like that before. I'm sure it was very "Halloween-like." He cried and wailed as if I had spanked him, but I didn't have to touch him! He changed his ways after the first correction and he never pulled on that curtain again. In fact, he always crawled or walked a very wide circle around it from then on.

That's how God wants us to be – easy to discipline with

a tender heart towards Him. It's not that He expects us to be perfect and never mess up. The blood of Jesus covers that. But we have to ask ourselves the following questions: "How receptive are we to God's direction and discipline? Are we sensitive to the guidance and conviction of the Holy Spirit?" That's what God was revealing in His invitation to the Israelites. Their acceptance or refusal of the invitation alone spoke volumes of where the people were and the condition of their hearts. If they saw no need for God in their lives and declined the invitation to return to Him, then their generation would repeat a history of disobedience and discipline. In such cases, pride would remain within and the relationship between God and His people would continue to be broken. Thankfully, the exile had brought humility to their hearts. That's a vital step in the process of restoration in which we shed all pride in exchange for humility.

Wholehearted Devotion

Not only was God allowing the Israelites to return, repent and start fresh, but He also asked them to evaluate their acts of devotion toward Him.

"He said, 'Tell the people of the land and the priests that when they fasted and mourned in the fifth and seventh months during these seventy years, it was not in honor of me. And

when they ate and drank, it was for their own satisfaction.'"
Zechariah 7:5-6

While the Israelites spent those seventy years in exile, their intended acts of devotion had become stale and stagnant. Every tradition they had to commemorate all that God had done for them as a people had become fossilized. I can relate, can you? It's hard to hang on to thankfulness. We can become cold and bitter in the deep winter of our trials. Our focus goes to how we've been hurt or what we have lost. Instead of developing an attitude of deep respect for God, we allow our selfishness to seep out and infect what should be pure and humble before Him.

The most beautiful depiction of wholehearted devotion belongs to Mary Magdalene. Mark 14:5-9 and John 12:1-8 reveal her selfless act of reverence. She is the one who poured an entire pint of very expensive perfume onto the feet of Jesus. Judas questioned why she did that, when it could have been sold to benefit the poor. Martha and others were busy making preparations for dinner. But instead of pouring herself out to everything and everybody else, Mary sat at the feet of Jesus. She didn't see the pouring of perfume as a waste. To her, it was a passionate offering. When she used her hair to wipe His feet, she didn't consider it making her hair messy or oily. It was a sincere act of adoration towards Jesus.

Paul gives us a good reminder in Colossians 3:23-24: "Whatever you do, work at it with all your heart, as though you were working for the Lord and not for people." That principle should play into every aspect of our lives. In our jobs, with our family and in rush hour traffic, everything we do should be out of a heart of worship toward the Heavenly Father. God deserves reverence, despite the gains or losses in this life. He is unchanging in His love for us. What excuse do we have that we cannot have an unchanging devotion to Him? If He never, ever does another thing for us, He still deserves all that we have for the rest of our entire lives, because of what He has already done. Period. The Israelites took this to heart and so should we.

Return, Repent, Redeem, Restore

God can do so many good things with a humble heart. Humility towards God leads to an overwhelming discovery of a bunch of "R" words. It's as if you're the special guest on Sesame Street that introduces all the important words that begin with the letter "R." Returning leads to repentance, repentance results in redemption, and they all lay the foundation for the work of restoration. If you look up the word "return" in the dictionary, you will see that it means to go back to a previous state or position.

But I am going to go out on a limb here and define what it is like to return to God, from my personal experience. It is a familiarity mixed with something new. It's like opening the door to a place you haven't been in a while and being greeted at the door with an overwhelming acceptance. You almost feel not worthy to enter, because of where you have been. You keep telling yourself that you are not dressed for the occasion, but warmth and such a rare expression of love embrace you into the doorway. Your heart has hungered and hurt for such relief that you cannot let go of the wholeness that has surged through you. In that moment, you realize all of the places that you have been before were the wrong places. This is where you belong, in the arms of Jesus.

That's what it feels like to return to Him. You become keenly aware of every single detail in your life. Good and bad, as well as right and wrong spill out of you and this conviction comes over you. It's not a pointed finger; and it is not a bad conviction. It's more of an awareness of the goodness, the holiness and the righteousness that has graced your presence. This overwhelming desire comes over you to pour your heart out, empty your pockets and wash your clothes. Now that you know what is good and right and pure, this is where you want to be. This is what it feels like to repent. You don't want to leave. You don't want to go back to where you came from, because for the first time in a long time you feel so many good things. His goodness overtakes your badness. His freedom releases your bondages. You feel cleaner, lighter and like new. Your imperfections are gone and all of your debts are paid in full. That is redemption. All of this, God does to reclaim our lives.

The beauty doesn't stop there. Once you have allowed the Maker of your heart to reclaim it, restoration can take place. Restoration, breathtaking, eye-popping, wondrous restoration, has only just begun. The dictionary defines restoration as returning something to its original state. However, flipping through the pages of God's Word, you will notice that God defines restoration very differently. In Joel 2:21-26, God declares He will not only restore that which was taken, but that He will restore it to the point where the harvest will be full and overflowing. Jesus declared, in Mark 10:29-30, "No one who has left home or brothers or sisters or mother or father or children or fields for me and the gospel will fail to receive a hundred times as much in this present age: homes, brothers, sisters, mothers, children and fields—along with persecutions— and in the age to come eternal life." In the days of Moses, when an ox was stolen, the offender had to restore the debt by giving five back. If a sheep was taken, then four were to be gifted back. And, after all the loss, destruction and turmoil that Job faced, God restored to him twice as much as he had before.

Are you getting the picture? But first, what was it that God requested from Job prior to his restoration? A prayer. That sounds simple enough. But Job had to swallow any pride and bitterness that he had and pray a humble prayer for those that hurt him. We are able to return to God only because He returns to us out of mercy. In His loving-kindness, He calls upon us and extends the invitation to return to Him, saying that He will return to us. By grace, He accepts us and we can start over, but it will not be the same. When God restores, it's bigger than before and it's even better than we anticipate it to be. Through repentance and redemption, our love for Him grows. And by restoration, our faith is multiplied.

Just as the Israelites discovered, it all starts with a humble heart toward the God among the myrtle trees, who declares: *"Return to your fortress, O prisoners of hope even now I announce that I will restore twice as much to you."* *Zechariah 9:12*

Prayer ~ *Thank you, Heavenly Father, for the invitation* to come back to You. I am in awe of the door that You open to repentance, no one can shut. You return to me with so much and I feel as if I have little to give. Teach me, God, how to live a life holly unto You. Even though I may come from a generation of people, like the Israelites, that have made it a custom to ignore You and harden their hearts – I want to break that tradition. I return to you, God. Even though this direction is unfamiliar, I know You are with me and will guide me. May your redeeming power be evident in every part of my life. Grant me, God, the grace to walk with You in wholehearted devotion and lead me into the restoration that is only found in You. ~ Amen~

Shades of Scripture

"I will restore them because I have compassion on them." Zechariah 10:6

"Let us then with confidence draw near to the throne of grace, that we may receive mercy and find grace to help in time of need." Hebrews 4:16

"He must become more important while I become less important." John 3:30

"Humble yourselves before the Lord, and He will lift you up." James 4:10

"And he said to them all, 'If you want to come with me, you must forget yourself, take up your cross every day, and follow me." Luke 9:23

"In him we have redemption through his blood, the forgiveness of sins, in accordance with the riches of God's grace." Ephesians 1:7

"I have swept away your offenses like a cloud, your sins like the morning mist. Return to me, for I have redeemed you." Isaiah 44:22

"I will give them a heart to know me, that I am the Lord. They will be my people, and I will be their God, for they will return to me with all their heart." Jeremiah 24:7

Chapter 6

DEATH BY DISCOURAGEMENT

"The Lord is near to those who are discouraged; he saves those who have lost all hope." Psalm 34:18

"The Christian life is not a constant high. I have my moments of deep discouragement. I have to go to God in prayer with tears in my eyes, and say, 'Oh God, forgive me' or 'Help me'." — *Billy Graham*

I have grown to love Easter Sunday. I mean, I liked it when I was growing up, but Christmas always won out as the favorite – and you can probably guess why. More than waking up to the smell of ham and deviled eggs, I love the deep-down affirmation that just seems to automatically come with the day. It's like a sweet token of assurance from God Himself that out of all the holidays to get excited about, this is

THE ONE. It's quite amusing when you think about Easter, however, that out of every time we go to church, that day just seems to run smoother. We go to bed earlier. We get up earlier. Everybody knows what they are going to wear and eat a week beforehand. If new shoes aren't part of the new Easter outfit, I'll go to the trouble of cleaning everybody's shoes (and let me just say I don't do that as often as I probably should). It doesn't matter what argument arises, how bad a hair day it is or if Jesus returns – we are going to church, taking Him with us, and we will be on time. Another Easter miracle is that no matter how late I stay up cooking the night before, I am somehow not sleepy during the service.

When the Israelites returned from exile, it was like an Easter Sunday morning. Excited and free, they set about their call to rebuild the temple. God was moving hearts – literally:

"In the first year of Cyrus, king of Persia, in order to fulfill the word of the Lord spoken by Jeremiah, the Lord moved the heart of Cyrus king of Persia to make a proclamation throughout his realm and to put it in writing:

This is what Cyrus king of Persia says:

'The Lord, God of heaven, has given me all the kingdoms of the earth and he has appointed me to build a temple for him at Jerusalem in Judah. Anyone of his people among you – may his God be with him, and let him go up to Jerusalem in

*Judah and build the temple of the Lord, the God of Israel,
the God who is in Jerusalem. And the people of any place
where survivors may now be living are to provide him with
silver and gold, with goods and livestock, and with freewill
offerings for the temple of God in Jerusalem.'" Ezra 1:1-4*

I'll bet they were high as kites! Not only was this
Persian king setting them free and returning all the items that
King Nebuchadnezzar had taken from the previous temple,
he was telling everybody to bless them! They had more
donkeys, unleavened bread and precious metals than they
probably knew what to do with. Sounds like a very perfect
Easter Sunday morning.

In Ezra 3:3, we're told that "despite their fear of the
people around them, they built the altar on the foundation"
first. But what do you think happens next? The same thing that
happens to us from one Easter to another: lots of discouraging
days in between. Ezra 4:4-6 goes on to tell us:

*"Then the people who had been living in the land tried
to discourage and frighten the Jews and keep them from
building. They also bribed Persian government officials
to work against them. They kept on doing this throughout
the reign of Emperor Cyrus and into the reign of Emperor
Darius."*

Can you even imagine putting up with that type of

sabotage, day in and day out, for one year? Not to mention sixteen years? They endured so much for so long, that I can only imagine what they were saying: "This must not be God's will. It's too hard! Such is life!" Isn't that what we all think sometimes? As we are gradually beaten down each day, the discouragement takes over and snuffs out that positive, moving emotion in our hearts that God once stirred up.

So why can't every day be an Easter Sunday? Well, it could be. It should be. Jesus's death, burial and resurrection are finished. Nothing changes that fact. Our personal circumstances do change, however, and can cause us to be distracted from that sobering reality. The sad truth is that we have a lot of spiritually down days where all we want to do is wear our holy sweatpants and put ourselves behind a closed door. Discouragement makes everything worse. Seriously, it's like having one of those horrible head colds when everything tastes bad and nothing smells good. From my own experience, I've realized that when I am discouraged, I am looking too much to everything around me. I'm in "me mode" – what's happened to *me* and how it hurt *me*. These are the times in which I have taken my focus off of Him.

After my mom's death, I walked around for a very long time feeling and acting defeated. I centered everything in my life on her death. It's crazy, isn't it? But I've noticed the tendency in others as well. It shows up in the ways we allow everything to gravitate toward our loss, our hurting and our disappointments. We somehow start living in defense of our discouragements and fearing further loss and hurt. We will have some very disheartening days, maybe even seasons. Jesus warned us of that. Before the events that led to the crucifixion He told the disciples, "In this world you will have trouble. But take heart! I have overcome the world." (John 16:33) That's where our hope is – in Christ's overcoming.

When God spoke to Zechariah, the Israelites were in what you could call an in-between Easter deadlock. All the discouragement they received carried them into a sixteen-year standstill. Zechariah overheard the angel's plea with God, saying:

"Lord Almighty, how long will you withhold mercy from Jerusalem and from the towns of Judah, which you have been angry with these seventy years? So the Lord spoke kind and comforting words to the angel who talked with me."
Zechariah 1:12-13

As Zechariah stood there, he received a fresh encounter with the God of Hope. At that time, Jesus had not been born of this earth yet. But God poured out the secrets of

His heart to Zechariah. He foretold the coming of Christ and revealed that He was going to "pour out a spirit of grace" (Zechariah12:10), and that "a fountain will be opened up to cleanse from sin and impurity" (Zechariah13:1). Those myrtle trees were the classroom for a New Testament Sunday school lesson for Old Testament times.   With discouragements, we were only meant to be visitors or passers-by, never meant to take-up permanent residence in depression. As believers, our hope is to be centered on Christ's resurrection and not our troubles. Our antidote for any obstacle or discouragement we could ever have in this life is the hope that is found in Him.

What confidence we have in Jesus! Our true source of hope comes from our relationship with Christ. It was among those myrtle trees where the change from discouragement to hope took place. It's where eyes shifted their focus from the impossible around them to the planned possibilities through God. We must open ourselves to the reassurance that if God cared enough to seal the deal – to write the last chapter of this book of life that we are in – then He cares for every intricate detail of our lives. In John 10:10, Jesus said: "I have come that they may have life and life to the full." Full means complete, full to the rim, sufficient, lacking nothing – that's what our lives can be and are meant to be with Christ as the centerpiece.

There are many things and people that we can place our hope and trust in, but in the end it will all return void. It may satisfy for the moment, but it will not be lasting. It's His mercy that shows compassion in our times of misery. And, like the Israelites, we must grasp that confidence and hold on to it, for it is our confidence in Him that lays the foundation of our faith. Every day we awaken, the celebration of Christ's resurrection should burn hot within us – stirring a passion for Him in everyone around us. As the old hymn goes: "My hope is built on nothing less than Jesus' blood and righteousness." He is our living hope.

Prayer ~ *God, I need You to take this discouragement from my heart. It is heavy with the weight of my past, the weight of what is ahead and the weight of this world. Everything feels so hard and impossible. Deplete me, God, of worry. Empty me of fear, Lord, and fill me fresh with You. Like Zechariah, I am in desperate need to know your kindness and your comfort. I know you are the only one that can give me what I need to go on. Open my eyes to your resurrection power. When it feels that all opposition is against me, let me feel the strength of You. Oh God, move my heart once again with a passion and zeal to live for You. You are my confidence and my encouragement. I ask that You give me a supernatural, unwavering confidence in You. May discouragement no longer cause me to question Your goodness, Your will and most of all Your love for me. Wake me up, God, with the hope and celebration of You. ~ Amen. ~*

Shades of Scripture

"Let us give thanks to the God and Father of our Lord Jesus Christ! Because of His great mercy He gave us new life by raising Jesus Christ from death. This fills us with a living hope." 1 Peter 1:3

"Through him you believe in God, who raised him from death and gave him glory; and so your faith and hope are fixed on God." 1 Peter 1:21

"We have this hope as an anchor for our lives. It is safe and sure, and goes through the curtain of the heavenly temple into the inner sanctuary." Hebrews 6:19

"Let us hold firmly to the hope we profess, because we can trust God to keep his promises." Hebrews 10:23

"You must also be patient. Keep your hopes high, for the day of the Lord's coming is near." James 5:8

"The Lord is all I have, and so in him I put my hope. The Lord is good to everyone who trusts in him." Lamentations 3:24-25

"And this small and temporary trouble we suffer will bring us a tremendous and eternal glory, much greater than the trouble. For we fix our attention, not on things that are seen, but on things that are unseen. What can be seen lasts only for a time, but what cannot be seen lasts forever." 2 Corinthians 4:17-18

"For everything that was written in the past was written to teach us, so that through endurance and the encouragement of the Scriptures we might have hope." Romans 15:4

Chapter 7

"So too, there is a remnant chosen by grace. And if by grace, then it cannot be based on works; if it were, grace would no longer be grace." Romans 11:5-6

"The law condemns the best of us; but grace saves the worst of us." — Joseph Prince

Imagine my excitement when another cat was found to add to our collection of strays (insert sarcasm). But, wait, let me back-up a bit and tell you the full story. We had been running a bush hog over an old pasture on our property. As my father-in-law walked across the field, he noticed movement among the piles of cut hay. He hesitantly approached, fearing that it was something struggling for life. Surprisingly, it was a warm, fuzzy, blood-free black kitten.

Somehow, it had escaped death by four, eighteen-inch-wide tractor tires and the four-foot-wide cutting deck of the tractor. Of course, I cuddled it and started counting appendages as if it were my own little baby. The only thing I noticed was the very tip of its tail, about the size of a sharpened pencil tip, had been snipped off. But there was no bleeding and you could barely tell it was missing. And you certainly can't tell now, as he has grown into a beautiful cat. I told myself that we were only going to keep him long enough to find him a good home outside of ours. That was before I realized there was an emotional attachment associated with bottle feeding little animal babies. My husband, the animal control officer of our household, couldn't turn the little survivor away either.

I've grown fond of the little guy walking around our house reminding us of God's grace and protection. He's our cat named "Lucky" – God's mascot for Matthew 10:29-31:

"Are not two sparrows sold for a penny? Yet not one of them will fall to the ground apart from the will of your Father. And even the very hairs of your head are all numbered. So don't be afraid; you are worth more than sparrows."

We would have named the kitten "Grace," but the males in the house wouldn't allow it. They said that was more of a girls' name. So to keep the peace, we girls obliged. Aside from using it as a pet name, I don't believe in being "lucky." Luck is more of a shoot-from-the-hip, haphazard belief in chance; whereas, everything about the Bible and God and the life, death and resurrection of Jesus revolves around the message of grace. Grace is superfluous favor. It is a gift that is given but not earned. Grace, in its very essence, is a God-ordained hope of survival. God's care and concern for us is hard to fathom. It's difficult to understand, because oftentimes we can't see it. All we see is this giant bush hog of life spinning around us with everything being uprooted and cut down, leaving us to feel as if we are taking our last breath. It's hard to realize when you're in the thicket of the tough times that He is the One who sustains. We feel like He's the one driving the tractor chasing us down.

Yes, I said that – it's time to be real. Haven't you felt that way? I think that's what God mostly wants from us – to be REAL with Him. We know that He wants a relationship with us. A real, intimate relationship is what God desires with each one of us. No fake stuff. We must also be real with ourselves. And for that to happen, He allows us to pass through some very difficult, seemingly lonely times, when there is absolutely no one else....but Him. And there is positively no other answer....but Him. Just like valuable gold, we are put into the heat with the intentions that the very pieces of us that remain after the trials and the testing are the real parts. Some of those real parts are good and some we could do without.

Phantom Pain

I never really understood pain until I went to nursing school, and even after that, I felt more clueless. Do you know what pain is defined as in the nursing realm? Pain is…. and I quote…. "Pain is what the experiencing person says it is." That's it. There's no deep, lengthy hypothesis to it. I could have a procedure done and come out with very little pain. On the other hand, you take someone of my age, gender and medical history and put them through the exact same procedure, using the same doctor and surgical technique and, even though they don't experience complications, they could still come out doubled over in pain. It is what it is to each person.

This lesson really hit home working one of my first night-shifts as a new nurse. I remember receiving my report of assigned patients and the look of relief on the face of the day-shift nurse as she passed on the Florence Nightingale torch to me. I barely had time to clip my pager to my scrubs and tuck my dosage calculation cheat-sheet into my lab coat, before I received my first call to a patient's room. Full of confidence and pride, I ran to the rescue of my patient. I popped through the door in my pristine, white scrubs and found my patient in obvious distress. He was sitting up straight in a flat hospital bed and fidgeting with everything within his reach. "He's confused," was the first thought that came to my mind.

I had left my patient notes at the nursing station, so I couldn't cull any guidance from those. I had to wing it, so I started asking questions and doing my robotic assessment. It wasn't long before, with his wife's help, I figured out he had been hospitalized for observation post-operatively and he was experiencing pain. "Okay, I can fix this," I thought to myself. Before I simply threw pain medication at him, I decided to take a peek at the surgical site to see if the pain was caused by something I could fix, such as a tight bandage or a bothersome suture. When I pulled the sheets back to assess his abdomen, the site of his recent surgery, he re-directed me to his left leg. I asked if that was where he was experiencing pain.

"Yes!" he all but screamed. "It's horrible and never goes away! My foot is throbbing and pounding!" Then he began to shake and to breathe anxiously.

"But sir, your left leg has been amputated, above your knee," I said. "And it looks like that occurred some time ago, because you have a healed scar."

He looks at me crossly and responded, "You may not see it. But it's there. I know it is, because it hurts!"

No truer words had been spoken to me. Ever. Others may have thought he was hallucinating, as I did at first, but I understood him. He called me out. This time, the patient schooled the nurse. I recognized what it was like to hurt from something you cannot see, to experience pain from something that no longer existed. Instead of my patient hurting from his most recent surgery, the trauma of an old injury haunted him. Many of us can relate to having phantom pain. It's an unwanted visitor that reminds us of the pain of our past. It's just crazy, the way I can look back at my struggles and see how I wrestled with my faith. I couldn't see faith the way I was trying to see it or I couldn't feel faith the way I wanted to feel it. So because I felt it didn't fit into this little clay pot of mine, I questioned its existence. Yet I continued to be tormented and in bondage over other things in my heart that were also unseen. I was folded over in pain from all the hurt, bitterness and resentment that could not be seen but could certainly be felt, just like my patient. Like broken clay pots, we can only be fixed by the Potter's hands. Just as He has allowed some elements of breaking to occur, He is faithful to mend. He can and will breathe life into our brokenness. Greater is He that is within us. We may not be able to see or feel the work of faith in our lives all the time, but others can.

"Yet we who have this spiritual treasure are like common clay pots, in order to show that the supreme power belongs to God, not to us. We are often troubled, but not crushed; sometimes in doubt, but never in despair; there are many enemies, but we are never without a friend; and though badly hurt at times, we are not destroyed. At all times we carry in our mortal bodies the death of Jesus, so that his life also may be seen in our bodies. Throughout our lives we are always in danger of death for Jesus' sake, in order that his life may be seen in this mortal body of ours. This means that death is at work in us, but life is at work in you." 2 Corinthians 4:7-12

The Four S's

Like "Lucky," David was found out in the field. In the sixteenth chapter of 1 Samuel, is written the account of the time when God sent Samuel to anoint the one whom He had chosen to be Israel's new king. Only God did not tell Samuel it was David he was looking for. He had given Samuel instructions to invite a man named Jesse to go with him to take a calf and make a sacrifice unto the Lord. That's all that Samuel knew. God was giving him step-by-step instructions. It was one of Jesse's sons that God had already chosen. It was up to Samuel to find him and anoint him. Upon arriving at Jesse's house, Samuel first approached a son named Eliab. This must have been a very good-looking guy, because at first sight Samuel thought that he was surely the one God had chosen. Shortly after that assumption, God tells Samuel:

"Pay no attention to how tall and how handsome he is. I have rejected him, because I do not judge as people judge. They look at the outward appearance, but I look at the heart." 1 Samuel 16:7

Jesse brought out all seven of his sons, one by one, with the same answer: "No, the Lord hasn't chosen him, either." Finally, Samuel asked, "Do you have any more sons?" Jesse answered, "There is still the youngest, but he is out taking care of the sheep." So Jesse went out in the field and returned with his youngest son. In walks this, what the scripture refers to, "handsome, healthy young man, and his eyes sparkled." The Lord spoke to Samuel, saying, "This is the one – anoint him!" That's the best part of the story. His eyes sparkled. He may have been the youngest one of the group and maybe not the most attractive of all the brothers, but he had the best heart, so much so that his eyes sparkled from it.

There are seasons of our lives that we may feel as though we are stuck off in some field somewhere. Feeling alone with nowhere to hide and no one to help us is like having a giant bush hog of life threatening our very existence. The field is a vast place where things get scattered, tossed about and cut down. Rather than a place that we meet our demise, the field can be a place to witness the grace of God. But we should not be looking at the pieces of ourselves scattered among the field and saying, "My God, you almost killed me!" Instead, we can say, "My God, by your grace alone I remain!" It's no mistake that somehow, someway we survived the heartache, grief and turmoil that surrounded us. Just as we are forgiven by His grace, we survive by His grace. But the point is that we are not called to be just survivors but the ones who thrive. He wants us to thrive. To look back on our hardest times and see that we somehow got through is an absolute miracle. So many times, passing the temptations to give up and give in is a praise that we can't give ourselves. We can't take credit for that. That's grace at its finest.

In Matthew 5:13, Jesus calls us, as children of God: "You are the salt of the earth." In verse 16, Jesus goes on to appoint His children: "You are the light of the world." As children of God, we are endowed with the ability to handle and digest everything that we could ever encounter in this life. This is not because of anything we have done or could ever do, but because of the grace of God and the gift of redemption through Jesus. In our good times, we are to let the light of Jesus shine within us. In our hard times, the light of Jesus should continue to shine bright within us. Resilience demonstrated through God's grace is what separates the children of God from the world. That is salt. Taking ups and downs stride-by-stride and maintaining love and trust in God the Father is an elegance that only comes with that intimate relationship He calls us to. That is light. How we handle our bush hog in the field experiences is not just part of our personal faith walk; it is God's heart to demonstrate His power through your life. As 2 Corinthians 2:14-16 says:

"But thanks be to God! For in union with Christ we are always led by God as prisoners in Christ's victory procession. God uses us to make the knowledge about Christ spread everywhere like a sweet fragrance. For we are like a sweet-smelling incense offered by Christ to God, which spreads among those who are being saved and those who are being lost. For those who are being lost, it is a deadly stench that

kills; but for those who are being saved, it is a fragrance that brings life. Who, then, is capable for such a task?"

The life of one living for Christ is meant to reflect Christ in every aspect, even to the extent of being a sweet-smelling fragrance. It feels like our circumstances and all those hurtful, tender parts of our lives define us. I once overheard someone say: "She hasn't been the same since her mom died." Which was true – I wasn't. And it wasn't a change for the better, it was for the worse. All these labels we walk around with: divorced, abused, abandoned, widowed, single parent – are like defects. No one asks for any of this. Jesus taught that life wasn't going to be perfect and that we would have tough times. Even though we don't understand why things happen or if He caused it, we do know that He allowed it. Rather than our circumstances defining us, God will use them to refine us. God is more interested in the condition of our hearts than He is in our circumstances. Whether those circumstances are good or bad, His heart is to bring us through them to be better internally than we were before. God revealed to Zechariah regarding His people:

"In the whole land," declares the Lord, "two-thirds will be struck down and perish; yet one-third will be left in it. This third I will refine them like silver and test them like

gold...." Zechariah 13:8-9

God refers to a remnant of His people throughout the Bible. The remnant is what's left after destruction. In the wake of chaos and upheaval, by the grace of God a remnant remains. The grace that allows a remnant to survive is the same grace that strengthens and restores. There are several places throughout the Bible that God refers to testing and refining His people as gold and silver. I did a little research on the process of refining gold. It was interesting to find out that the refining part came *after* the process of smelting. In smelting, the gold is put through a furnace of about twenty-one hundred degrees Fahrenheit. The gold must be melted before its impurities can be removed. Did you understand that? It must be put to the heat FIRST, before any of the undesirables are removed.

God sees us as precious treasure more valuable than gold. We, too, are tested in the furnace of affliction. It is in our hardships that our faith in God is measured. And it is when personal calamity is experienced that our confidence in Him can be analyzed. Pain and anguish, whether it's physical or spiritual or financial or emotional, the form it comes in is very hot and extremely uncomfortable. It is by God's grace that we are not consumed. He pulls us out of the fire or turns down the heat so that we are not overtaken by it. Rather, we are melted down to a point that all the undesirables are exposed in an effort to remove them. Things that you don't realize exist within you, such as bitterness, anger, disbelief, resentment, envy and such, tend to grow larger during suffering. And that's just exactly what God desires to happen, so He can cleanse us in the refining process.

We can choose to see our afflictions as punishment and bad luck, or we can see ourselves for what we really are: survivors by the grace of God. After grief and torment, trauma and loss, we remain a remnant chosen by grace. We must not allow our past or present circumstances to devalue our worth. And because God wants to clarify and purify our hope and faith in Him, there is no room for the impurities. They pollute our purpose and weigh us down. By His grace, we survived and will continue to survive. In the process of our refinement, while we are out in the field and as we pass through the Potter's hands, we are to be shiny, salty, smelly and sparkly for His glory.

Prayer ~ *Oh God, help me to see this field that You have me in as a place of preparation rather than a place of demise. Give me eyes to see that I am not alone and that You are with* me. *Confirm in my heart, God, that when everything around me seems to be falling apart that You remain in control. When it feels as if a bush hog has lost control in the field that I stand, grant me the faith to know that it is You who sustains me. Through Christ old things have passed away and the new has come and I praise You for that! By your grace alone, Lord, I survive. Thank you God, that it is your divine plan to refine me and perfect me. By Your sovereign hand and Your wondrous works, God, you make me a new creation. ~ Amen ~*

Shades of Scripture

"And I will test the third that survives and will purify them as silver is purified by fire. I will test them as gold is tested. Then they will pray to me, and I will answer them. I will tell them that they are my people, and they will confess that I am their God." Zechariah 13:9

"I am your God and will take care of you until you are old and your hair is grey. I made you and will care for you; I will give you help and rescue you." Isaiah 46:4

"But now, for a brief moment, the Lord our God

has been gracious in leaving us a remnant and giving us a firm place in his sanctuary, and so our God gives light to our eyes and a little relief in our bondage." Ezra 9:8 "In that day the Lord Almighty will be a glorious crown, a beautiful wreath for the remnant of his people." Isaiah 28:5

"I myself will gather the remnant of my flock out of all the countries where I have driven them and will bring them back to their pasture, where they will be fruitful and increase in number." Jeremiah 23:3

"But I will leave within you the meek and the humble. The remnant of Israel will trust in the name of the Lord." Zephaniah 3:12

"See, I have refined you, though not as silver, I have tested you in the furnace of affliction." Isaiah 48:10

Chapter 8

"No one can please God without faith, for whoever comes to God must have faith that God exists and rewards those that seek him." Hebrews 11:6

"I hate to see complacency prevail in our lives when it is so directly contrary to the teaching of Christ."

— *Jimmy Carter*

I'd like to make a nomination for a new inductee into the lineup of Biblical heroines. Right there among Queen Esther, Ruth and Deborah needs to stand another. The trouble is I don't know her name. All I know is that she suffered from a bleeding issue for twelve years. Through that course of time, she tried everything and spent all she had for some type of relief. Nothing helped and her conditioned worsened. You can read her faith resume' in Mark 5:25-34 and Luke 8:43-48.

As a nurse, I find myself guessing what her hemoglobin and hematocrit values might have been with that type of long-term blood loss. It's certain that her anemia would buy her several days, if not weeks in the hospital, along with multiple blood transfusions and countless tests if she were with us today. To have lost blood for that long a time, she must have been exhausted. She was probably short of breath just getting out of bed after a long night of tossing and turning.

Imagine what went through her mind when she heard about Jesus, and her hopes and fears collided. It's as though I can hear her say, "Just one more try. I must go see Him." How she gathered the strength to put her clothes on, I'll never know. I can picture her walking the trek from her house grasping onto anything she passed to help hold herself up. Her body must have been telling her she couldn't go any further, but her spirit was telling her to keep walking toward Jesus. Because she had never seen him before, her internal GPS was telling her to just follow the crowd. But her battle wasn't over; she had to conjure up the energy to get through the multitude of people who were crowding around Him.

Her plan was to just touch the hem of His garment. I can picture her dropping to her knees and crawling to Jesus, being pushed and kicked the entire way. Then she gets to where she is able to stretch out her arm and grab the very edge of His robe. Scripture says she immediately felt in her body that she was freed from her suffering. And, at that moment, Jesus asked, "Who touched my robe?" The disciples thought that was an odd question, because there were so many people crowded around Him, but Jesus could tell a difference in her touch, which was one of effort and desperation. What gall it must have taken to keep going! But, despite all the hurt, suffering and discouragement, she didn't stop until she found Jesus.

Unlike my biblical heroin, I was at the opposite end of the faith spectrum. I kept waiting on everyone's prediction of "It will get easier with time" to come into play. At about the eight-year mark after my mom's death, I realized everything was still the same. Grief had carried over into my life that long and was just as strong as the day she died. One would have expected things to become easier after that amount of time, but it felt as though my life was still tormented by grief. It was as if I had hit the pause button and was still waiting on things to resume as normal. Essentially, every aspect of my life seemed to be paying some sort of price. My marriage, job, health, finances, you name it – my suffering took a toll on all of them at some point. I continued to search for relief from my heavy feelings, but counseling, medication, nothing worked. It was then that I realized I had been grieving not only the death of my mother, but also the death of God in my heart. When I chose to turn my back on God and allowed my heart to shift away from a love relationship with Him, I essentially chose death. I didn't realize His presence until I experienced His absence.

When the Israelites stopped work on the rebuilding of the temple, their relationship with God was neglected. They no longer put Him first, so all parts of their lives were affected. After being defeated by discouragement, they settled into a life of what was considered normal by their opposition. Maybe that's where the saying "If you can't beat 'em, join 'em" came from, because that is exactly what they did.

Zechariah 1:8-11 reads:

"During the night I had a vision – and there before me was a man riding a red horse! He was standing among the myrtle trees in a ravine. Behind him were red, brown and white horses.

I asked, 'What are these, my lord?'

The angel who was talking with me answered, 'I will show you what they are."

Then the man standing among the myrtle trees explained,

'They are the ones the Lord has sent to go throughout the earth.'

And they reported to the angel of the Lord, who was standing among the myrtle trees, 'We have gone throughout the earth and found the whole world at rest and in peace.'"

When you first read that, you might think, "Rest and peace is a good thing!" That's what I thought, too. But, actually, they were in a place of complacency, which is a dangerous place to be. The Israelites had become okay with being okay. Their state of complacency was their dead-end destination, due to their abandonment of faith. That's the danger – being comfortable when you shouldn't be. That's what complacency is defined as: living in a feeling of quiet pleasure or security, quite unaware of potential danger. The Israelites were in desperate need of God. The trouble was they didn't realize it.

Not-So-Happy Camper

While we are searching for God, it sometimes feels like we are in uncharted territory. And most times, we are. However, just because it is unfamiliar, does not mean that God has not directed us down that particular path. Uncharted territory is the best place to be, because we must rely on God to get us through it. It's in those times that we have no choice but to draw close to Him, which is just where He likes us to be. We tend not to like those times in our lives, because we look at the physical aspect of things where everything is unfamiliar and uncertain. This means we have become too comfortable with the familiar. I believe, however, that God really looks forward to introducing us to uncharted territory.

Those times of wilderness are like camping trips to Him. He's thinking, "Oh, boy! I get to go camping with my kids!" And we're thinking, "Oh, no! Not camping again!" We think about all the doing without and "roughing it," when God only sees opportunity for some one-on-one time, a chance for Father-to-child intimacy. He sees a period of total dependence on Him with everything else left behind. He wants to show us His survival skills and how He can make water come out of a rock and light a bush on fire (with no matches, mind you). He wants to surprise us by pulling the ingredients for perfect S'mores out of His backpack. Sure, I like a hot shower just as much as the next person, but to witness showers of grace in the toughest of times....that's where it's at.

God wanted the Israelites to go on a little camping trip with Him, too. He sent the invitation through Haggai:

"This is what the Lord Almighty says: 'Give careful

thought to your ways. GO UP INTO THE MOUNTAINS and bring down timber and build the house, so that I may take pleasure in it and be honored,' says the Lord." Haggai 1:7-8

But the Israelites didn't want to go. They were comfortable where they were. Their enemies were now their friends and everything was, in their eyes, better than ever. They had established a common ground with their accusers and began to focus more on their own houses and crops, which was complacency at its best. God called, but they were at rest and at peace right where they were. They weren't just kicked back in a recliner, they were busy, but busy doing the wrong things. God points out that their efforts and energy were in the wrong places.

"The Lord Almighty said to Haggai, 'These people say that this is not the right time to rebuild the Temple.' The Lord then gave this message to the people through the prophet Haggai: 'My people, why should you be living in well built houses while my Temple lies in ruins? Don't you see what is happening to you? You have planted much grain, but have harvested very little. You have food to eat, but not enough to make you full. You have wine to drink, but not enough to get drunk on! You have clothing, but not enough to keep you warm. And workers cannot earn enough to live on. Can't you

see why this has happened?'"

We can't stay where we are. Whether it's a place of hurt or a place of self-satisfaction, we cannot stay. If we do, then we choose to self-heal and self-satisfy. Why would we even consider selling ourselves short like that, when we could keep moving with God? I'll tell you why. It's because we fear being hurt more and experiencing added disappointment. We fear rejection and loss – the very roots that lead us to where we are. And it's because we accept our brokenness and allow it to make us who we are. Oh, to be more like the heroine without a name, and to be less like the Israelites who were more interested in making a name for themselves. How wonderful it would be to get to a point where we count the costs of NOT running to Him, rather than worrying about how much it costs running toward Him!

Did the heroine question herself? Did she ask, "What if I don't make it to Jesus? What if I can't find Him? What if my body fails me before I reach Him?" Maybe. But her actions overrode her questions, threw her into a faith drive and caused her to ask another question: "What if I *don't* go to Him?" Her fear of being content in misery was enough to keep her hungry for healing. May we never have to be in a state of physically bleeding to realize we need Jesus and keep us on the search for Him. And may we never, ever be satisfied in and of ourselves. We can't just sit and wait (like I did) for everything to suddenly be okay. Yes, the Spirit comes to us and comforts and brings peace and ministers to us. But what are we to do? Are we to sit in our homes suffering internal bleeding? Do we roll over when we feel defeated and take up the lifestyle of our enemies? Quite the contrary.

Faith is As Faith Does

It's a big step back into faith. It's almost like saddling a horse that you have fallen off once before. Maybe not the best comparison, but you get the feeling, right? It was a big fall. You were all kinds of sore for a long time. You hurt in places you didn't even know existed. The fall left you scared and with the conviction that you would never get back on again. I remember the first time I decided to get back in the faith saddle again. I had no other choice and I was desperate. I am convinced that God set it up that way. I remember my first prayer after six years of vowed silence towards God. It was awkward, filled with choppy words and sweaty palms. "Please, God, help me. I cannot.....lose again." I was pregnant with our first child. Up until that time, I felt in control of everything. Then, all of a sudden, in pregnancy, you are so not in control of anything. Your emotions, your body and even the baby inside of you, all are outside of your full control. You can be under the care of a doctor, eat right, exercise and do everything you are supposed to and still have complications.

The fear of loss rocked my world. Are you hearing me? I said ROCKED it. So much so, that I decided to give this "God business" one more try. So I gave up control of assigning control to other people and things and just gave it all to God. I turned from a mime to a gum bumper, overnight. I'd wake up praying. Throughout the day, I would pray. I would sneak off to the bathroom at work to pray, because I felt those silent prayers inside my head might not be as effective. I wanted God to hear me. Do you know how hard that is for people like us to declare and believe in divine healing and health even though it didn't happen for our loved one? To decide to keep talking with God, even when we don't receive an immediate answer? But God supports us all the way. He knows our weaknesses and gives us strength to overcome them. He is well aware of our ability to make the wrong decisions, but when we lean on His wisdom, we won't make them again.

That's where God wanted the Israelites, and that's where He wants us, getting up from where we fell and moving closer to Him. He wants us to be constantly seeking and searching for Him, trusting that He will move on our behalf. Like the heroine, we should never be satisfied with anything or anyone this side of Heaven but Him. She had to push through the crowds that circled around Him. Today, it feels like we have to push against a crowd that is going the opposite direction of where we need to go. If we haven't found Him, it's because we aren't looking. God's Word declares that if we seek Him with the entirety of our hearts, then we will find Him. May we be found searching for more of Him each and every day, never growing cold or stagnant.

Gather your strength and start walking toward Jesus. May you keep pushing and pushing through the crowd until you are close to Him. Continue to press in and when you have done that, press in even more. Reach out further and further to touch His heart so that He turns and says, "Who touched me?" In response to His turning, you rise and say, "I touched you. I need you." Your timid faith transforms into a powerful testimony when He responds, "Your faith has healed you. Go in peace and be freed from your suffering."

Prayer ~ *Forgive me, God, for being comfortable when I need to be moving with You. Forgive me for allowing other things and other people to rob my affections for You. Help* me to never be satisfied with anything other than You and your will for my life. Give me the spiritual strength to keep looking, keep searching and to continue to press in for more of You. Help me to realize, every second of every day just how much I need You. Grant me a faith, God, that stirs my life into a permanent action toward You and for You. In Jesus name, ~Amen.~

Shades of Scripture

"At that time I will search Jerusalem with lamps and punish those who are complacent, who are like wine left on dregs who think, 'The Lord will do nothing either good or bad.'" Zephaniah 1:12

"For the waywardness of the simple will kill them, and the complacency of fools will destroy them." Proverbs 1:32

"I know what you have done; I know that you are neither cold nor hot. How I wish you were either one or the other! But because you are lukewarm, neither hot nor cold, I am going to spit you out of my mouth!" Revelation 3:15-16

"I will destroy those who have turned back and no longer follow me, those who do not come to me or ask me to guide them." Zephaniah 1:6

"Seek the Lord while he may be found; call upon him while he is near" Isaiah 55:6

"Sow righteousness for yourselves, reap the fruit of unfailing love, and break up your unplowed ground; for it is time to seek the LORD, until he comes and showers his righteousness on you." Hosea 10:12

"You will seek me, and you will find me because you will seek me with all your heart." Jeremiah 29:13

Chapter 9

"And just as all people were made sinners as the result of the disobedience of one man, in the same way they will all be put right with God as the result of the obedience of the one man." Romans 5:19

"The bottom line in the Christian life is obedience and most people don't even like the word." — *Charles Stanley*

I would do it if it was necessary, but I am thankful that it's not. There is a reason that I exist in this present time and not in the era of animal sacrifices. I could not do it. I am one of those who stop to pick up worms and put them back in the grass. You know the worms that are washed onto the sidewalk after a hard rain? I have been known to plow into a ditch to avoid hitting a squirrel and to stop traffic in order to move a turtle out of the road. I'm a sucker when it comes to animals, especially ones that are sick or injured. There's something in me that wants to help them, not hurt them. With that being said, I'd have a lot of unpardoned sins if it was left for me to slaughter a baby lamb.

The first mention of an animal sacrifice can be found in the book of Genesis after the disobedience of Adam and Eve. After the flood, Noah made an offering of clean animals. In the days of Moses and throughout the Old Testament days, such acts were customary in atonement for sins. When the Israelites escaped from Egypt, God gave them the instructions on building a tabernacle. It moved with them as they journeyed to the Promised Land, a specific place that God would inhabit and make His glory known. It was also where the sacrifices were made. As the Israelites settled into their promised homeland, King David had it in his heart to build more of a permanent place for God to dwell. When the throne was passed along to David's son, Solomon, so was the assignment of building the first temple. This was the same temple that was destroyed in the Babylonian takeover. What would you guess were God's first instructions to His people upon their return to restore Jerusalem? It was the main channel that brought them closer to God: the temple.

I wonder: When God asked the Israelites to rebuild the temple were they intimidated? Did they go through some type of performance anxiety? The former temple was built by King Solomon and it had gold everywhere. He had unlimited money and resources available to him to build it. With the Israelites, however, that was not the case. When they returned from exile, they were given supplies, but that was nothing compared to what Solomon had at his disposal. Who can compete with that? They were already discouraged by all the people who were hired to plot against their efforts. Add in a little building envy, and you can see why the Israelites were frozen in fear.

Among the myrtle trees, God addressed their issue:

"Who despises the day of small things? Men will rejoice when they see the plumb line in the hand of Zerubbabel."
Zechariah 4:10

The "day of small things" refers to the way in which they interpreted their lives, which was small and insignificant. They began to believe that their best efforts resulted in nothing. But God kept telling them, through Zechariah and another prophet, Haggai: "Be strong. Do not fear. I am with you." So they stepped out in obedience and started rebuilding the temple. As the walls were going up and everything started coming together, they began to wrestle with the significance of it. What did God say about that?

"Who of you is left who saw this house in its former glory? How does it look to you now? Does it not seem to you like nothing?" Haggai 2:3

As the temple neared completion, I can just picture the ambiance as the people examined their soon-to-be finished project. They tilt their heads and close their eyes halfway in effort to see it a little more…..I don't know, HEAVENLY. And the sound of a whoopee cushion (or that game show sound when someone misses something – "Wha-wha-whaaaa") would be a fitting sound effect to describe how the people viewed their offering to God. But God could read their hearts and continued to encourage them to be strong, to have no fear and to keep working, because He was with them. Then He goes on to make this promise:

"The glory of this present house will be greater than the glory of the former house." Zechariah 2:9

Did you catch that? Despite the fact that their rebuilt temple looked like a shack compared to what Solomon built, God's glory upon it was going to be greater. Why? Because of God's goodness in regard to their obedience. You see, it's not about us. It's all about Him. Little truly is much when

God is in it. We are called to be obedient and the rest is up to Him. This is the result of our not asking a whole lot of questions, trying to rationalize and figure everything out, but simply walking in obedience through faith.

Thy Will Be Done

Blessings are directly related to our obedience to Him. It's always been that way and it always will be. God had spoken to the Israelites through Zechariah and Haggai about why they were experiencing a life of lack. It was because God's house, the temple, remained in ruins. Essentially, it was a reflection of their disobedience. The twenty-eighth chapter of Deuteronomy lays out the definition of a life of blessing and one of curses. It is like an ingredient list for each type of life. I will be honest and tell you that I recognized things from my life out of both the obedience definition and, scarily, the disobedience definition, too. It was made clear to me where God had been good to bless me and where my disobedience to Him had brought some unfortunate things into my life. I encourage you to read Deuteronomy twenty-eight and allow the Holy Spirit to speak and reveal it to you, personally.

Our willingness to obey God is a vital sign of our

restored faith in Him. How do we walk in accordance to God's will? How do we keep those running shoes in the closet? Jesus gives us the answer in Matthew 6:10:

"Your kingdom come, your will be done on earth as it is in heaven."

The Lord's Prayer is one that has trended to the side and been replaced with our own prayers. Those red letters need to be uttered from our lips each time we pray and to remain on the forefront of our hearts. Obedience to His kingdom, obedience to His will – for everything to line up here with us, right now, this very moment, just as it does in heavenly places. Our heart cry should be similar to what Jesus prayed: "Not my will, Lord, but your will be done." The Israelites experienced their own heaven on earth when the temple was completed. Their obedience and submission to God's will created a source of honor and praise among them. His splendor overflowed the temple in a way they had not previously experienced. And to think, they would never have obtained that on this side of heaven, if it weren't for their obedience.

Because Jesus submitted to the will of the Father, we have much to be grateful for. Sacrificing animals is no longer necessary, not now, not ever. Jesus lived a perfect life of obedience and gave it all to redeem our disobedience. The very moment that Jesus died, everything that separated us from God no longer existed. When the Lamb of God took away the sins of the world, the veil was torn, making communion with the Heavenly Father a reality. More than inhabiting temples and tabernacles, God wants to inhabit our very lives. No matter how dirty and rickety our little shack is, as long as we build it in obedience to Him, He will restore it and fill it with His glory, more now than ever before.

Prayer ~ *Heavenly Father, thank you for Jesus. Thank you for the gift of salvation. Thank you for life. Help me, God, to walk in obedience to your will for my life. Cause me to see your will for me with significance and purpose. Much was given for me, and for that I am grateful. May your kingdom come, may your will be done on earth as it is in heaven. Enable me to be strong, to be fearless, and to work and know that You are with me. I want to experience your greater glory.* ~ *Amen* ~

Shades of Scripture

"Don't you know that your body is the temple of the Holy Spirit, who lives in you and who was given to

you by God? You do not belong to yourselves but to God; he bought you for a price. So use your bodies for God's glory." 1 Corinthians 6:19-20

"I appeal to you therefore, brothers, by the mercies of God, to present your bodies as a living sacrifice, holy and acceptable to God, which is your spiritual worship. Do not be conformed to this world, but be transformed by the renewal of your mind, that by testing you may discern what is the will of God, what is good and acceptable and perfect." Romans 12:1-2

"Because God is always at work in you to make you willing and able to obey his own purpose." Philippians 2:13

"Trust in the LORD with all your heart. Never rely on what you think you know. Remember the LORD in everything you do, and he will show you the right way." Proverbs 3:5-6

"God has made us what we are, and in our union with Christ Jesus he has created us for a life of

good deeds, which he has already prepared for us to do." Ephesians 2:10

"Surely you know that when you surrender yourselves as slaves to obey someone, you are in fact the slaves of the master you obey—either of sin, which results in death, or of obedience, which results in being put right with God." Romans 6:16

"We have, then, my friends, complete freedom to go into the Most Holy Place by means of the death of Jesus. He opened for us a new way, a living way, through the curtain—that is, through his own body." Hebrews 10:19-20

Chapter 10

"We are never defeated unless we give up on God."
Ronald Reagan

"If you read history you will find that the Christians who did most for the present world were precisely those who thought most of the next. It is since Christians have largely ceased to think of the other world that they have become so ineffective in this." — *C.S. Lewis*

All good defenses start with a strategy. This was ours: "Defend yourself, and we'll go get ice cream." This may not have received the popular vote for the best parental advice, but my husband and I felt it was. Our oldest son had some issues with bullying in his second- and third- grade school years. We had gone through all the proper channels of reporting the bullies and the incidents to the teacher, which would help for a time. But we would soon find ourselves in a threat-received position.

"What if I get sent to the principal's office?" he would nervously ask.

"Well, you might. There is not supposed to be any fighting at school," I replied. I remember the expression on his face throughout the whole conversation, as if he had been sentenced to life without parole or something of the kind. "What other option do you have? We can't pull you out of school and run from the problem."

I then began rationalizing out loud with our thirty-year-old son in his nine-year-old body. "This guy knows when to pick on you. He waits for a time when no grown-ups or witnesses are around. He does just enough to torment you, but does not hurt you badly enough to leave evidence. Then it becomes a 'he said, he said' battle between the two of you." I laid it all out there for both of us in hopes we could rationalize more clearly. "I hate that it has come to this," I said. "But if you don't prepare yourself, then I'm afraid we're fighting a losing battle." We both paused for a moment to study each other's game face.

Then he suddenly stated his decision for defense,

"Okay, I'm ready. What do I do?"

Over the next few days, his dad taught him several defense tactics and they practiced different scenarios for their use. Finally, he not only felt ready on the inside, but he also appeared ready on the outside. He was no longer hesitant about going to school or looked for excuses not to go. He was ready. He was past the point of wavering on what to do and when to do it. He was set. As he walked to the car, I no longer saw a questioning, stumbling little boy full of fear. This confident, poised young man had emerged with assurance. As we sat in the line of cars in front of the school, he talked through different scenarios and how he would respond, and sought my approval.

I encouraged him and as we parted, I reminded him of our three basic principles. "One: Don't go looking or asking for trouble. Two: Be ready and prepared if trouble comes to you. Three: If he gets physical with you, give him a good pop to break free and go report the incident to your teacher."

He began to get nervous again and asked, "But what if I get sent to the principal's office?" I sent him off with a wave and these final words: "You will not be in trouble at home for defending yourself. We will go get ice cream."

Offense vs. Defense

We prayed and considered every Bible verse when we were handling our bully issues. In fact, 1 Peter 3:9 kept coming to mind: "Do not repay evil with evil or insult with insult," which totally contradicted our parental advice. And let's not forget all the school rules and regulations that would haunt the rule-following mom in me every now and then. However, it was time that our son learned to stand up for himself, because Mommy and Daddy could only do so much. Then an epiphany – a "What Would Jesus Do?" moment – occurred. With a few key words in mind, I Scripture-hunted and Googled until, poof! There it was in Matthew 10:16:

"I am sending you out like sheep among wolves. Therefore be as shrewd as snakes and as innocent as doves."

This was just a small piece of the advice that Jesus gave the twelve disciples as he sent them out into the world. Of course, I realize that my son is not a disciple, and the other little boy is no wolf. But Jesus' words give direction for our strategy when facing any opposition. He was charging them to be as keen and defensive as a snake, yet harmless and non-threating as a dove. To have all of the attributes of a snake could end in deception, and to have all of the attributes of a dove would be considered weakness. It requires a mix of both to make such a rare breed....something I like to call a "snove.".

Following this charge in Matthew, red letters highlight the page as Jesus sends the disciples to their duties of driving out evil spirits and healing the sick. He goes on to warn them to be on their guard. He cautions them about being arrested, flogged, persecuted and just down right hated because of Whom they represented. Why on God's green earth, would He tell them all of that? Is He trying to talk them out of being disciples? Was it a scare tactic? Never. It was for the same reason we gave our son the advice that we did: to prepare and equip them for the fight of faith. Our son's biggest issue was that he was surprised. Therefore, he responded in a scared and defenseless manner. Jesus didn't want that for those He appointed to walk in His anointing. He wanted them guarded *and* ready, "snoves." Interestingly, the next time my son and the other young man crossed paths at school, there were no bullying issues. Expecting opposition and being prepared to take a stand against it was a deterrent in itself, not to mention the assurance and confidence my son received through the experience. All in all, it ended with a good reason to celebrate with ice cream.

What would you do if you heard some very critical,

potentially threatening news? Would you share it with others that needed to know and come up with a game plan? Or would you avoid the details for fear of creating chaos? I'd like to think I would choose the first, but I don't much like to be the deliverer of hard news. The benefit of Jesus foretelling others about the hard road ahead was intended to be a faith builder just as much as it was to prepare them.

When we put the advice of Jesus into play in our faith in Him, we are able to move from a position of defense to one of offense interchangeably. The fight of faith calls for both. Just as in a game of football, our defense is our frontline protection from the opposition. As Christians, our defense is the shield of faith. We must hold onto our faith, for it is what extinguishes the flaming arrows of the enemy. If we let go of our faith as we have done in the past, we will be overcome by the opposition. But everybody knows it's the offense that has the ability to score, because they have the ball. Likewise in our faith, it is when we maintain possession of our faith that we have the ability to move and make advances in our individual lives and for the Kingdom of God.

Nehemiah demonstrated this logic very well. After the Israelites experienced opposition in rebuilding the temple, they learned the tactics of their enemy. They incorporated their own "snove" strategy and after the second attempt, the new temple was up. They had come a long way, but they weren't finished. The walls around Jerusalem remained in rubble. The city walls were a first-line protection against thieves and enemies. Without those walls, not only were the Israelites vulnerable to attack, but the broken wall was a symbol of disgrace among God's people. Nehemiah was moved into action, but he knew from the history of the restoration that his assignment required strategy. With "snove" quality, he set out at night to inspect the city walls. Other than a few men that he took with him, he told no one what God had laid upon his heart. After planning, restoration commenced, with everyone working on the part of the wall that was nearest to their home. Just as expected, they were mocked and ridiculed and received word of a coming attack:

"They all plotted together to come and fight against Jerusalem and stir up trouble against it. But we prayed to our God and posted a guard day and night to meet this threat." Nehemiah 4:8-9

They didn't run away, however. They didn't question their purpose or God's love for them. Neither did they question God's existence because of their troubled times. They prayed. Then they posted guards to meet the threat. Because Nehemiah was guarded and anticipated such threats, he positioned people at the lowest points of the wall and any area that was exposed. They were prepared to fight with swords, spears and bows. Once the enemies learned of Jerusalem's preparations and that God had frustrated their plans, the Israelites were able to return to their work of restoration. Did they turn their backs? Oh, no. They learned from their previous experiences with the enemy. The Scriptures say that half of the men worked while the other half posted defense with spears, shields and armor. Each worked with a sword at his side. Those who were required to carry materials did so with one hand and held a weapon in the other.

Overcomers

That's where faith does its best work, in the darkest of times and in your weakest moments. Having faith doesn't mean that life is going to be easy and that everything good comes to you. Faith means that in the very worst, saddest and most painful of circumstances, your trust in God is not shaken. Faith is essentially the trust we place in God to give us what we need and to provide what we don't have. In faith, your belief in Him is not moved. Your salvation through Christ is not questioned and, therefore, your relationship with

Him does not fade. Faith is an attitude of the heart. It means walking in a direction that He leads and knowing that He will take care of everything, even the things we cannot see or figure out for ourselves. It sees God at work and trusts in Him rather than physical evidence. Faith is a gift. It provides security and removes fear. But, most of all, faith is a shield. It's built for the fight.

The reconstruction and restoration of Jerusalem was complete. The temple was rebuilt from the ground up and the strong wall around the Holy City was restored. More than a place of worship or a barrier of defense, the Israelites' faith in God had been tested time and time again. In the end, their faith in the One True God was proven and they were victorious because of it. Despite the times of unfaithfulness and sins of the people, God had proven His love for them through discipline and His love through restoration. As with the Israelites, our way to victory comes through realizing that we have an opposition to our faith, but mostly that our faith in God is a fight worth fighting and a ground worth standing. The season of running is over. Our strength comes from what the run proved within us: that our love, worth and restoration come from Christ alone. Enough of being bullied! Too long have we allowed our security in Christ to be threatened, the hope we have in Him to be mocked and our trust in God to be ridiculed. No longer shall we allow ourselves to question our spiritual heritage in Christ Jesus. Spiritual compromise on our behalf would be choosing defeat. It is time to stand on the security of God's gift through Jesus Christ, to quit running and get in the fight. The advice from Hebrews 6:1 seems quite fitting for us runners:

"Let us go forward, then, to mature teaching and leave behind us the first lessons of the Christian message. We should not lay again the foundation of turning away from useless works and believing in God."

It's time to fight the good fight. We've been given our own "I can't pull you out of school and run from the problem" advice. In the book of Revelation, Jesus revealed the "spiritual bullies" to the seven churches. Each church had its strengths and each had its weaknesses, or as Jesus said: "I have this against you." Just as he did in the Church of Ephesus, He is aware when we have lost our first love for Him. He knows when we turn to other things that take the place of Him. That is considered idolatry, the same thing He found in the church in Pergamum. At the end of each message to each church, Jesus would say: "To him who overcomes…"

It is our turn to wake up, repent and strengthen what

remains within us. Even though we live where Satan has his throne, we must remain true to the name of Jesus and never renounce our faith in Him. It is in His name alone that we can persevere and endure hardships without growing weary. For God to send His only son, Jesus, to die on the cross for our sins, how much more would He have to do to prove His love? Isn't that enough to stand on and fight for? Or do you still feel like such a love doesn't exist because you simply didn't see it with your own eyes? Is that what we've come to as a generation, not believing God's message and truth simply because we didn't SEE Christ crucified?

I know I am asking a lot of questions. Sometimes the best answers are within the questions. The generation of Israelites in Zechariah's day, I'm sure, asked themselves some very similar questions. "What if we keep going the direction we're going? Maybe it's a dead end for a reason? God has revealed Himself to us among the myrtle trees and offered restoration, what more could we ask for?" And let's not forget Thomas, the disciple who happened to not be with the other disciples when Jesus appeared after His resurrection. When they shared of the good news, he replied, "Unless I see the nail marks in His hands and put my finger where the nails were, and put my hand into His side, I will not believe." (John

20:25) It took Jesus coming into a house, regardless of the locked door, and appearing to Thomas, saying:

"Peace be with you! Put your finger here; see my hands. Reach out your hand and put it into my side. Stop doubting and believe. Because you have seen me, you have believed; blessed are those who have not seen and yet have believed."
John 20:24-29

Stop doubting and believe! Blessed is our inheritance, and I do not mean just gifts, as in monetary or physical gifts, although, God can and does bless His people in those ways. More to the point, we are blessed that He is our victor and He is our shield. So have faith in Him. The battle is His. The crown of life is the reward of a faith that is faithful even to the point of death. To those that obey His will to the end, He will give authority over nations. It is the finished work of Calvary that allows us to be considered worthy to be written in the book of life, never to be blotted out. A gift of the morning star and the honor to be acknowledged before God the Father and His angels is an honor through grace. And all of this, He offers to a runner, a sinner or whatever you are. No one is worthy of such – absolutely no one. You are worthy simply because He sees you through the finished work of Christ Jesus. Expect obstacles and opposition along your life of faith. Be prepared to stand and fight, knowing that He has already declared victory over you. Hold on to what you have so that no one takes your crown. In the name of Jesus, you are an overcomer and He is your great reward.

Prayer ~ *Oh, God, you have brought me so far from where I once was. I ask that you continue to restore my faith in You alone. Strengthen what remains within me so that I can stand for what is rightfully mine through Christ Jesus. Direct my running toward You, God, so that I will live a life of abandoning everything that is not of You. I am humbled by how You never left my side. Place the shield of faith firm within my grasp, never to let go, and to be victorious in fighting the good fight of faith. By your grace, God, I am an overcomer.* ~ *Amen* ~

Shades Of Scripture

"Above all, taking the shield of faith with which you will be able to quench all the fiery darts of the wicked one." Ephesians 6:16

"Who shall separate us from the love of Christ? Shall trouble or hardship or persecution or famine

or nakedness or danger or sword? As it is written:

"For your sake we face death all day long; we are considered as sheep to be slaughtered."

No, in all these things we are more than conquerors through him who loved us. For I am convinced that neither death nor life, neither angels nor demons, neither the present nor the future, nor any powers, neither height nor depth, nor anything else in all creation, will be able to separate us from the love of God that is in Christ Jesus our Lord." Romans 8:35-39

"There is nothing in us that allows us to claim that we are capable of doing this work. The capacity we have comes from God." 2 Corinthians 3:5

"But have reverence for Christ in your hearts, and honor him as Lord. Be ready at all times to answer anyone who asks you to explain the hope you have in you, but do it with gentleness and respect. Keep your conscience clear, so that when you are insulted, those who speak evil of your good conduct

as followers of Christ will become ashamed of what they say. For it is better to suffer for doing good, if this should be God's will, than for doing evil." 1 Peter 3:15-17

"Be ready for whatever comes, dressed for action and with your lamps lit." Luke 12:35

THE END

Need Additional Copies?

To order more copies of

Among the Myrtle Trees

contact NewBookPublishing.com

❏ Order online at:
NewBookPublishing.com/Bookstore or

❏ Email Info@NewBookPublishing.com